STEPS

in
Self-Knowledge

Leddy and Randolph Schmelig

Unity Books
Unity Village, Missouri 64065

CONTENTS

LEARNING THAT GOD IS LAW:

LEARNING RIGHT JUDGMENT:

FACETS OF SELF-UNFOLDMENT:

Steps in Self-Knowledge

A LETTER
ABOUT BEGINNING . . .

Dear Friend in Truth:

It may well be that the steps in Self-knowledge particularly carved out for you are not far away in some distant mountain range, in some mysterious place, with some rare mystic teacher. It may well be that the steps in Self-knowledge that have been awaiting your footsteps are close and familiar. The steps you need to take begin where you are; they are mapped out in your own daily route between the usual and common places you travel to and from each day. They are the steps around the rooms you now inhabit, steps in the office or shop you walk about in day to day. These very steps, taken with spiritual direction, are as full as any of sanctity.

Every saint or sage of the past or present day has walked about his or her rooms or house or village or city, just as you walk now in your own usual places. You walk with the same rhythm, the same energy, the same pauses, the same longing.

Start with the very next move you make to step with faith and power toward that same excellence these shining ones have reached. Hold the thoughts, *wholeness, peace, abundance, wisdom, mastery, joy,* and the path to your highest goals will unfold before you.

You too are one of those "shining ones." You too are a saint, a sage, a master in potential. The mountaintop, the monastery, the prayer garden, are the places where you stand now, the atmosphere you breathe. In your heart of hearts you know the Truth that you are indeed an "anointed one." Go forth, fresh from the baptism of that great idea, to begin.

As you go consciously on this path, the blessings of all lovers of Truth everywhere in the cosmos go with you. All of these friends in Truth welcome you to the path and urge you to begin quickly. Yet do not be hurried as you travel. It is our hope that you will take a long time to read these simple lessons, and that you will *use each practice exercise for a full month's time,* pausing every day to sit alone in the same quiet place while you study and practice.

And it is also our hope that you will begin a Spiritual Diary, a private textbook of some kind that you can carry, wherein you will write down your own thoughts and experiences on the spiritual path. Let this be a record of the spiritual mastery you attain, a reminder of the steps in Self-knowledge that you are taking.

Above all, it is our hope that you will *take*, with confidence and gladness and peace, the numberless steps in Self-knowledge that expand before you in this blessed life experience. For as you attain each step in your own Self-knowledge, you gain the bliss of spiritual awareness, and you lead the world to God-realization as no other can.

Blessings!
Leddy and Randy Schmelig

Learning to Relate
A FIRST STEP

As you initiate this month's study, it may be that you are more and more aware of the personal commitment you have made and the purposeful direction of will that keep you actively on this path. You have chosen this way to find out yourself, for yourself, the Truth. The privateness and quietness of this inner pursuit may at times give rise to a certain feeling of loneliness. If this has been the case with you, recognize it honestly for what it is, yet look beyond the surface of the somewhat negative aspects to the truth about the experience. The sensation of loneliness is common to all serious Truth students now and then;

do not fear it or allow it to shake your strong foundation in spiritual understanding. And do not let this feeling of loneliness upset the emotional or outer balance of your life. The feeling is only temporary— it will pass. While it lasts, it is better to think of the experience not as an aching and unproductive loneliness, but as a growing, cleansing time—even a necessary time of aloneness. This is the indication of that special way in which each one is alone, and yet no one is alone.

Aloneness . . . the word might be better understood, paradoxically perhaps, as "all-one-ness," for each and every individual has already found or will undoubtedly come upon this feeling at one time or another in life. This life, with all its turns and lifts and valleys, is really all one, however many separate individuals may appear to be living it. The many are really all one.

Lesson 1: All-one-ness

The very aloneness that you encounter at times on the spiritual path is not really new, is it? Have you not felt a kind of aloneness all of your life? As a child without playmates on a long afternoon, or even surrounded with playmates, did you not feel it tugging at you even then? And now, alone in your home, or away from home, or even surrounded with family and loving friends, do you not sometimes for a moment pause in the midst of the celebration and reflect on how alone you really feel?

Take heart—what is it you are so lonely for? Is it a real friend, a real love, a real family, really belonging? But even when all of these blessings are yours, isn't the longing still there? It is right that you should have these feelings sometimes. It is the Lord that you feel so lonely for. When you are feeling most alone, perhaps then you are nearest to the consciousness of His immediate presence. He is calling to you, reminding your forgetful mind of its eternal Companion.

The Lord is the friend, the lover, the husband, wife, father, mother, child, sister, brother, confidant that you feel so lonely for. But the joyous reality is that He is here. He has not gone away for the weekend, or for a month or years or forever, leaving you here. He is right here with you now, as if to smile and reach out to tap your shoulder, saying, "Beloved, do not fret, *here I am*."

What do you think is happening when you read words that another has written and a wave of acknowledgment floods your mind with light? Does it not seem that God working through that writer has written the words just for you?

What do you think is happening when a child reaches out and touches your face, or a stranger, handing you your dropped parcel on the street, happens to brush your arm, or a loved one silently places his hand on yours in a gesture full of meaning? Does it not seem that God moving through each of you is recognizing, blessing, loving the God nature in the other?

Here it is, then, that "touch" again, that contact that is somehow the very foundation of the universe.

This is what all the poets and artists and teachers and philosophers and ministers are really trying to tell. You see, the most intense training and education and study in any field, at any institution, can only serve to indicate and emphasize and elaborate upon what each person everywhere already believes and experiences every day.

What do you think is happening when your glance happens to match the glance of another—even a person with whom you may never exchange words or physical contact of any kind—and a light wave of recognition somehow passes between you? Shopping at the grocer's with other people passing you in the aisles and exchanging looks with you; going by the window of the office and looking in at the office workers who look back momentarily; silently walking past the door of the hospital room as the pale face of a patient you do not know looks up at you for a second; seeing the faces of the children at a birthday party, and they turn and see your face—you are discovering that "relatedness" of all people in every kind of circumstance. You do not have to have words for it. You feel it in a touch, a thought, a word, and you know that it exists. You know in your heart of hearts that the God-life, the God-essence that is active in you is active in and through all, making all one.

The ideal must ever be to serve that God-essence in all. Somehow in this loving and selfless contemplation of all these expressions of God—of all these "selves"—one loses the limitations of the narrow self and gains Selfhood. You can feel, as the thought in the inspired writer's mind flows out to you through the written word, that your own mind rushes out and worships at the divine contact. You can feel, as the innate, ever-restless-to-express quality of love flows naturally out through the touch of another, that same quality rushing out through you to worship at the contact. You can feel, as you look into the faces, and see into the eyes of people, and they into your face and your eyes, that the God-intelligence is rushing out through each of you—even slipping out without your knowing what is taking place—to worship at the contact.

Because this process takes place through experience with others, it is quite right to worship through acts of brotherly and sisterly love. Bless the individual who calls upon you for aid of any kind, for through granting that aid, you attain freedom and help him to do the same.

When formal meditation seems almost impossible, go out and worship Him in your fellow beings. You see, there is no excuse for not worshiping the Lord, for He is to be found everywhere, in everyone. Even when this study place that you have so sanctified by your longing to know the Truth, and so blessed by your experiences of the presence and nature of God, becomes hard to come to; even on those days—and they will come now and then—when you cannot seem to take your place here and begin the discipline of this study, go out and perform that discipline in loving ways to people. The form of worship is not so important, after all. But whatever you do, worship. For in seeking Him, in loving Him, you attain peace and bliss indescribable. Continue these studies in that assurance, and do not fail to carry the attitude of adoration into the world. He is everywhere, all the time, and in everyone waiting, to be known.

The discipline of meditation is necessary, and a good and loving life of action and service is also necessary. Jesus Christ, spiritual Master, has taught: "You shall love the Lord your God with all your heart, and with all your soul, and with all your mind. This is the great and first commandment. And a second is like it, You shall love your neighbor as yourself" (Matthew 22:37-39).

That second commandment is like the first for the reason that the Lord is the very Self of yourself. Beholding and loving Him in others, you see Him in His full glory, and the self of you is also revealed as that very Self in essence. These are the two ways to see and know God. Seeing Him one way, you will see Him the other. What a wonder this is, and how full of joy the realization that the real miracle in life is His eternal nearness!

Think for a moment of a person you love more than words, more than your own life. How dear the nearness of this person is! Is there a food that tastes as sweet or satisfying as that nearness? Is there a diamond or an automobile or a mansion as desirable as that nearness? Is there a mandate in all the world as great as the power to be near this person? Then think of the nearness of the Lord, who is all love, all peace, all joy, all good. It is the distillation of Him that expresses as all that you adore in your loved ones. This Presence is near to you now, in every particle of the universe, activated in the looks and movements and words and personalities of people everywhere, once you know how to look for Him. Know the Truth: you cannot be alone. You *can* be consciously "all one" with the cosmos, all one with Him.

Practice Exercise

Become still now and center inward. Draw the mind back, back, back from the world of appearances, toward the source of all Truth within. As you draw close to that inner light, know that all over the world, consciously or unconsciously, others are nearing that light of Truth that shines within their being. Many others are using this very exercise with you this very day and night. A bond of living light joins you, energizing and blessing each with power and freedom; enfolding each one in a halo of love.

Truly, you are bathed and cleansed and purified by this atmosphere of light and love. The very air is charged with comfort and peace and wholeness. You breathe light and love in and out as you breathe.

Become more aware of your breathing, even as you read. Let your breathing become even and satisfying. As you breathe in and out, think that you are inhaling the same light that surrounds all others in this vast universe. Consciously know for yourself and all others:

I take into my being the light and love of Spirit;
I give forth into the world only light and love.

Become even more still than before, and contemplate these ideas for a moment.

This same life-sustaining, consciousness-uplifting atmosphere that enfolds you now enfolds all beings everywhere. It enfolds this and all other worlds in the universe. You are sharing light and love and life with those dear to you, the others who live in the same place with you, those you do not know well and only pass by in life, and those you may never meet; with people younger and older and the same age as yourself, in every kind of place and situation there is. You share light and love and life with the earth itself and all the bodies of water, with all the trees and small plants, with the creatures easily seen and those that are microscopic dwelling among the leaves, with every form of life, known and (so far) unknown.

You share light and life and love with the cosmos. You are breathing with the allness of the universe, and it is as if you can hear the words coming from within you and coming from everywhere: "You are one with Me, and I AM one with you . . . all one."

Immerse yourself in this consciousness for a long, long moment.

This atmosphere of light and love that you are becoming intensely conscious of now is really the underlying nature of all things everywhere. There are no spaces in it; there is no breach, no pause in the living pulse and rhythm of divine life. Have you thought at one time or another that there was some place where God was not? Have you thought at one time or another that there was some person whom God was not indwelling? You know that this cannot be, for as you unfold spiritually you become consciously at one with that "breathing" or Spirit that goes on at all times, in every place, in every individual. Spirit is always quietly breathing light and life throughout the universe regardless of the outer manifestations. It sustains all there is without rest or qualification.

Think for a moment of a child blissfully sleeping in deep, deep sleep. The sweet form moves ever so subtly as the child breathes ever so evenly, ever so quietly. You may have to look twice to notice that there is any breathing at all, so deep and peaceful and still is the slumbering child. Yet when that child awakens, how unmistakable is his energy and vitality! Omnipresent Spirit breathes light and life continually, yet when the mind becomes alert to that universal life, when the consciousness wakes up like the child who has been deeply slumbering, you become dramatically conscious of the life-giving breath that has been going on all along, even when you were not aware of it.

The entire cosmos appears to be in deep sleep, like the child—yet that old rhythm is going on in every atom, in every living thing, in every person. Think of this regular, unceasing, free flow of Spirit that is interchanged eternally, shared from being to being, equal to all and infinitely abundant. See that all people everywhere are now beginning to wake up to that reality, stretching and rising up to energetically and vigorously undertake their spiritual identity and purpose. This *is* happening—it is happening to you right now!

As you sit very still, yet are alert for the beginnings of a new sense of relatedness with the universe, keep aware of the pattern of your breath. Read the remainder of the exercise, pausing to follow the suggested procedure. Then follow the pattern of inhaling and exhaling with the words given once again, only with eyes closed. Give yourself over wholly to the experience Spirit has for you, for the awakening to the life and light of Spirit.

Inhale slowly and deeply, without tension or much effort, as you think the words,
   You are One with Me.
Then exhale slowly, deeply, and easily as you think the words,
   I Am One with You.
Once again, inhale as you hold this word in thought for a sustained moment,
   All.
And then exhale slowly as you hold this word in mind,
   One.
Pause to let the feeling of the words move through your being, cleansing and freeing your thinking and feeling.

Remember that the capital letters indicate reverence and acknowledgment of the divinity of all who take part in this eternal interchange of light and life. Think of the affirmation as a kind of equation involving you and all people everywhere, you and the visible and invisible universe, the spiritual Self of you

and the Lord—God, the good omnipotent, omniscient, omnipresent.

How the limitations of regret and resentment and
loneliness drop away! If you will make a practice of
using this affirmation, along with the breathing pattern given here, often during each day this month,
wonderful results will come through for you. Use the
exercise even in the midst of activity, for perhaps this
is the best time of all. Through seeing Truth even in
outer activity, you activate the presence and nature
of the Lord in your world. Make note in your Spiritual Diary of the indications of unfoldment and
spiritual awakening that you perceive this month in
yourself, in those close to you, and in the world in
general. Never mind negative appearances as re-
ported in news media or seen on the streets. Spirit is
ever breathing light and life unceasingly, and more
and more the world is awakening!

Learning to Relate
A SECOND STEP

How fantastic it is that every turn on this pathway of self-discovery presents something new and vital! Truth does not gather dust like books on a shelf, but is ever active, moving, alive, *like people.* Schools and institutions will forever be under construction or in the process of being torn down, opening doors or closing doors. Even the greatest teachers come and go, leaving each student—properly enrolled or self-appointed—to find out things for himself.

The treasure is not to be found in print or in a lecture or a lesson. Words can only echo its splendor. Can words really tell what is in the most casual look passed from one traveler to another? This treasure is somehow in the makeup of those travelers; it may be enveloped by forgetfulness, but it is there just the same. And you know that the treasure is in you, growing as new wisdom and as deeper, fuller love.

Wherever you notice an expression of love in the world, look to its source—then deeper to the Source of that source, and you will find the treasure: God, the Truth, the essence of all life and all religion.

How can real religion ever be dry? If you find it dry, go and be refreshed in the love that others have for you and for one another. This is religion—God in action. When you find religion dry, return in prayer to that inexhaustible spring of eternal love and wisdom that overflows at the center of your being. Only one taste will reveal that the same living water flows within each individual. Look well into the human heart, for the Truth you seek is all there.

Lesson 2: Beholding the Light

If you are hungry, you must break the hard shell of the nut in order to taste the inside. So long as you let the nutmeat stay within the unbroken shell, you shall remain hungry. As long as you leave the treasure of spiritual identity undiscovered and untapped within yourself and others, you shall remain lonely and unfulfilled.

To realize the Truth and attain that satisfaction which is at the base of all joy, one must bridge the gap between what is said and what is actually believed and done. The goal of the sincere Truth student is not merely to learn about God, but to realize oneness with God. Realization implies the activity of making a positive change in consciousness, a change that will transmute all life experience in a positive way.

Once the goal of God-realization is consciously accepted, it is not so difficult after all to begin to change the consciousness and reshape the personality so that the way is easier and happier. More and more, you begin to genuinely share in the happiness of others, to rejoice in their good, feel compassion for their suffering, and indifference toward their mistakes. These simple rules of conduct will become a natural way of life for the spiritual aspirant, for God is love. As His nature is realized and expressed, love shines forth from the aspirant like a great light, illumining all.

When others around you find happiness and plenty in their life, it may often call forth your resentment instead of joy. The success and achievement others experience may call forth feelings of envy instead of rejoicing. The suffering others endure and the mistakes they make can easily call forth criticism and condemnation instead of love and understanding. When these tendencies of mind become apparent to you, recognize them as obstacles and begin at once to dissolve them with love and spiritual practice.

The illumined individual is like any other, with one important difference: he has made a decision about what he will permit to enter his consciousness; he has made a choice between the positive and negative sides

of life. Instead of finding fault in others, he has chosen to seek out what is fine and beautiful.

If you cannot honestly see others as perfect in
essence, perhaps it is because you cannot yet honestly
see yourself as unselfish, pure, eternal, perfect in
essence. If something has happened in your life experience to dim that self-image, try to lose that self in
thoughts of others. If you can lose yourself in the
thought of another for even one minute, it will
change your life, but the pitfalls are still there. Many
believe that they feel compassion, when they are
really drenched in self-pride over their own piety.
Many think they feel love, when what they feel is
largely possessiveness. Many believe they feel adoration, when they seek only their own pleasure. But
these tendencies can be overcome. The capacity for
the highest, purest love is innate in each person. That
same pure light shines, no matter what colored
shades are placed over it. The light still filters
through. And when the glory of that light is allowed
to shine forth unimpeded, how great is that light!

You must be willing to peel off the veneer of self-
righteousness, conceit, and self-importance before
you can approach God indwelling others. When this
has been done through keeping the mind on God in
prayer and in everyday duties, you can peel away
from your mind the veneer of selfishness or weakness
or imperfection that *you* see in others and behold the
Christ light in them.

It is not necessary to pretend that the actions of all
people are right and good. There is obvious wrong in
this world—even wickedness. Yet even more real,

though more subtle, is the underlying goodness. This goodness can come forth. The beginning of a new world is your own recognition of an ever-perfect potential and a sincere expectation of the expression of love. By your own growing love for the world, you are changing things.

It is true that some individuals or certain actions of many individuals may still signal negative emotions in your mind. Your spiritual unfoldment does not remove you from the usual sensibilities of the human race. You will still feel things; perhaps you will feel things even more intensely than ever before. Yet at the same time, as you grow in the certain knowledge that you and all others are in essence pure and eternal spiritual beings, emotion does not penetrate, but remains on the surface of your awareness. A flash of anger, though sharp, shall be like a mother's anger at her beloved child. It lasts only a moment, is activated only by the most loving and tender concern, and is forgotten as quickly as it appeared. Learn to be as forgiving as a small child. Learn to forget seeming wrong as quickly as possible. Children often seem so intent upon joy, upon things going well, that a moment's conflict is gladly forgotten so that play can go on. Look at life this way. How wonderful to be so delighted with life and the company of others that most conflicts can be joyously overlooked and forgotten, so that the play of life can continue. When things are harmonious and joyful, what great progress can be made by all on the spiritual path!

In order to realize this harmony, you must forgive. To forgive another is simply to accept him as he is, though not necessarily as he appears to be. If it seems impossible to forgive or relate to some particular individual, think of that person here with you now, studying and praying with you. Cut away in your own mind the mask of pettiness, vindictiveness, weakness, or cruelty that you have seen, and behold that person as he or she truly is—at peace, all love, all understanding. For in the heart of hearts, each one is seeking Self-realization, just as you are now. Beholding them in this way, how foolish seem hatred and resentment and fear! What a waste of time! How gladly you forget the appearances so that the joy of God-realization can proceed!

Many a young girl has suddenly awakened to her own beauty and blossoming womanhood at a sincere compliment from another. You can signal a new awareness of grace and joy and freedom in others by honestly and openly making known to them that you see them as happy, beautiful, and free. What is keeping you from doing this? Nothing of any importance. Seek the freedom of others as earnestly as you are seeking your own—then you will be free.

There was a certain student of Truth in India long ago whose guru (spiritual teacher) gave him a mantra. (A mantra is a special thought-centering and mind-freeing formula imparted in the form of a divine name or statement of Truth, meant just for a particular student at his own particular place in unfoldment. Through meditating on the mantra, the spiritual aspirant can make great strides toward God-realization.) The teacher made one important stipulation as he gave the mantra to the devotee: he warned him that if he told the mantra to anyone else, that person would immediately gain complete spiritual freedom while the devotee himself would be damned. After leaving the presence of the guru, the devotee at once gathered a large crowd about him and shouted the mantra to all who would hear. His teacher was greatly pleased.

Dwell on that unselfish love! The truth that the teacher no doubt wished the student to understand is that self-centeredness and the desire to place oneself first in all things is the only real "damnation" there is, for it means ultimate separation from unity with God, who is within all people. Through expressing love in the highest way possible, the spiritual aspirant is freed from all limitation. Through receiving love in the highest way possible, all persons attain God-realization. Get selfish concerns out of the way, for wherever they exist in your thinking, they are in your way.

Are there people who seem cruel and hard to you? Very well, God is disguised in many aspects of this world. Yet He is here, and His will is to liberate all people from the bondage of ignorance. Even through what may seem the most heartless and destructive act of another, you can get at the heart of the Truth that awaits in the experience. Forgive. Do not give in to the negative appearance. That mistaken concept—not a person—is your only true enemy. Yet, even that enemy is overcome with ease when you love. Real love has a way of beholding things as they are and of translating appearances into beautiful Truth. Therefore, cultivate love for the Truth and love for the true nature of all people, and Truth will reveal itself to you in beautiful ways.

Are there persons who appear to be indifferent to you? Never mind—the universe may appear to be indifferent, even callous. Yet your presence in this universe, on this planet, in the nation where you are living, in the particular region, in the time and space you occupy at this instant, affects the entire universe; and the universe is responsive to you, in turn, in subtle ways. The circumstances in which you find yourself, this body, this life, this era in history, these people around you—names known and unknown—with whom you have even the smallest interchange, have together called you into being in this very time and place through a collective order that can only be rightly defined as *love.*

This world with all its faces and forms has been lonely for you. The world has been longing for you; it needs you now. The perpetual urge of the universe is to know you, to know itself, and for you to know it as it really is: God manifest.

The goal is not self-delusion—far from it! The goal is not to put a rose-tinted veil over the eyes and pretend that the world as it appears presently is manifesting absolute perfection. The death of a friend, or some physical defect in a newborn child, or even the first drought or frost of the season would destroy that pretense at once in the rational mind. *The goal is to break free of delusion* and find out the essential perfect nature of things. You begin to see that this perfection is even now coming into view, regardless of the "setbacks." The trend of things is ever toward this perfection. The goal is to behold this one changeless reality, the Truth universal, inevitably to be known and expressed.

Each person that you can see with the eye or think about contains that same perfection. Think of stepping across the distance of all space, of spanning all time, past and present, to stand directly in front of each person, to look him or her directly in the face and behold the child and manifestation of God. Just as surely as Jesus Christ is the Son of God, each one of us is the son of God in essence. This potential may be unrealized or even unsuspected, but you can see it—not simply imagine it or hope that it may be there. You can behold the Christ light shining and delight in that radiance.

Practice Exercise

To conserve energy, many people turn off the lights in areas of their homes that are not in use at that time, and illuminate only that area where there is activity—the area where light is really desired. Meditation is also a form of conserving energy, not in the sense of withholding, as much as in the sense of redirecting all energy to the center of being.

Begin your quiet time now, by becoming still in mind and in body, and by focusing your attention on the inner Christ light. Sense a light at the center of your being; feel its warming glow radiating from within you outward. This is the one light that is really desired—the Christ light.

In order to do this effectively, begin to "turn off" the other lights in your consciousness. Is there some part or aspect of your body temple that seems to be in discord? Is there some health challenge, or discomfort, or nervous habit that seems to be continually drawing your attention from the area of desired activity? Does it seem almost like a neon sign flashing at the corner of your consciousness? Turn off this light, consciously, now. Gently and firmly withdraw the energy that is being wasted there and conserve it for the intense activity of spiritual unfoldment. You may want to say to yourself, *I now redirect this energy to the center of Christ light within.* More simply, say, *Peace! Be still!* The change in your use of life energy can be redirected only by a thought. Take a moment now to be intently still, and use what works with you to achieve this stillness.

As you cut off the current of energy in all areas but the one where the intense activity is taking place, you experience a surge of power in the inner Christ light. The Christ light suddenly flares into new fullness, filling the area of apparent discord with its warm healing glow. No energy has been wasted, only redirected to new heights of power.

Having achieved a certain degree of peace and readiness for spiritual experience, see whether there are any unnecessary lights still burning in your consciousness, in the mental realm of fear, worries, doubts, or anxiety over anything or anyone. This is perhaps the most difficult part, but positive results in this phase of the exercise are the most rewarding. Take a deep breath and set out resolutely to turn off the unwanted lights flashing in your thinking and feeling nature. Is there some grudge or hurt you have been holding that is constantly drawing your attention, wasting your energy? Turn off its light, pull its plug, and again experience a warming, illuminating surge of power in the Christ center of light. Take a long moment—there is no hurry. Although it does seem that effort on your part is required, it is an effort of *release*. See the energy of your being channeled to the Christ light. Behold and feel the Christ light healing that area where once energy was wasted. New peace and understanding are flooding your entire being now.

Each time the light is turned out in a problem or questioning area, or in a corner where a persistent negative thought has remained, the Christ light grows in dimension and intensity. The answers are coming through now, and they will become clearer and brighter. You are renewed in body, mind, and spirit. Affirm knowingly:

The Christ light illumines me, and I give thanks!

In this final part of the practice exercise, retain your awareness of light, as with your mind's eye you visualize a clear summer night sky. You can almost feel the sweet night air and see the stars overhead as pinpoints of light. The stars vary in intensity and nearness, yet each is a point of light. These lights are as countless as the people in the world. Think that they are the people in the world—each radiating the same Christ essence.

You may feel the tendency to give thanks once

again for the joy of this recognition. As the feeling of joy and thankfulness grows in your awareness, the light increases. And if you can keep the image of the sky full of stars in your mind, you can imagine each one growing more intense, reaching out to the light of your own being. The rays of each pinpoint of light spread and reach to touch all others. The sky in your mind's eye is all light and you are one with that light. Hold the feeling.

Affirm for yourself and for all others:
We are one in the Christ light.

Pause, and let that illumining peace fill your being. Out of the love and thanksgiving of your own consciousness, the words shine forth: *One in the Christ light!*

No words are really needed to elaborate on this great awareness. Only your experiences and new discoveries, during this month of practice, can make it even more real and wonderful for you. You are blessed as you give and receive ever-greater love, at one with the universe in the Christ light.

Learning to Relate
A THIRD STEP

You are moving forward to new horizons in your self-unfoldment. As progress is made on this path, you soon realize that the truly great moments you experience, the most striking realizations you encounter, come in the form of feelings. The revelation of Spirit seldom comes in the form of specific facts. Most of time your revelations come by way of a changed or uplifted attitude, a new orientation to all of life, and it is in applying this higher attitude that specific answers come.

As you proceed in learning to relate, a transformation in your attitude toward life is already surfacing.

You are experiencing a new affinity with all creatures, radiating a new warmth to all with whom you come into contact. Others are beginning to respond to your new understanding and uplifted consciousness. Many are especially attracted to you and calmed by your very presence. The challenges you meet are overcome more easily through love. The love that is active through you soothes the struggles of others. The peace and enlightenment of the whole world is helped through you as your heart is opened in love.

The feeling that is awakening in you is not really new at all. You have felt its warmth many times in your life experience in varying degrees. This feeling of oneness with all life that is developing in you is familiar, easy, comfortable, and natural. There is a simple word for it: *love.*

Lesson 3: Freeing the Flow of Love

You are a radiating center of divine love, a pure love that neither binds nor restricts, but frees and blesses all it touches. Love is the key to right relations with your sisters and brothers of this world, for all are your sisters and brothers in Truth, and love is the key to spiritual realization.

It is love that joins the elements of the universe, that charges all beings with life, that works all miracles. Through an awakening in your consciousness to the flow of divine love in and through all, you are led into a realization of the underlying unity of all life.

The master plan for Self-realization, the most direct path to your goal is this: love God—both as transcendent, omnipotent Principle, and as the immanent God-presence in all people. If you can learn to apply the love for God that you feel growing within you and direct it toward the divine center of every being, your own self-unfoldment will take care of itself, and you will greatly aid the progress of others. Put love first and the elements of your life will follow naturally. To tell a true lover of God that he must meditate, study, and lead a good, loving life and express only the Truth is absurd. His reply would be, "How can I do otherwise?" Express this love, let it shine, and your life will be an eternal prayer of joy and thanksgiving.

It has been taught in great religions of all places and times that in order to attain the ideal, one must be pure. Nothing is more purifying than love. If love is genuine, its expression and the results it brings will always be pure and good. Learn love, and purity will come. Pray for more love for all others, free of the limits of so-called "merit." Pray unceasingly for more intense love for God. Through grace, the love of God in action, the mind and heart become pure and the spiritual ideal is attained.

It also has been taught that the goal of religion is reached in an attitude of noninjury toward the world in general, and toward living things in particular. If total understanding and expression of noninjury in every phase of life does not seem reasonable or attainable to you now, never mind the details: pray for love. True noninjury is not produced by outer aus-

terities. True noninjury is a natural outpicturing of
the love that grows within the heart of the devout
Truth seeker.

It also has been taught that truthfulness is necessary to the spiritual life. This may seem ever so simple, but without the development of love in the consciousness, it is impossible to demonstrate absolute
truthfulness in all things in life. Therefore, love again
is the answer. Love absolutely, and you will speak
only the truth and act according to Truth at all times.

Be pure; practice noninjury in all the ways that suit
your nature; be truthful in your dealings with others.
Never forget that love is the very heart of these
qualities. God is love, follow Him, open your mind
and heart to Him, and your life and actions also will
follow Him.

Spiritual aspirations ever whisper to the sincere
Truth seeker that the ego must go and the loving
God-self must emerge. In this spirit, it is natural that
all desire to prevail over others in an egoistic sense
must go. All desire—even the slightest—to control or
harm others must go. Cover these negative tendencies
with love, purify them with love, and translate them
with love. The energy that would have been expended
in covetousness, resentment, or anger need not be
lost—only rightly directed. Move toward God-
realization with all the same fire and momentum!
Love is the opposite of the negative feelings; it is the
antidote and more. Pray for more love every day;
yearn to love in the purest, most selfless way. This
prayer is always answered.

Ah, the spiritual life! It is ever so free. Take from

it only what you will, give to it only what you will. But law is at work here, too. You cannot progress on the spiritual path without reaching a consciousness of harmlessness, compassion, and pure love. Look into the lives of saints and sages; each one is an example of the highest ethics. Strive to be fair; resist taking any wrong advantage. The phase of your mind that has been called your "conscience" will tell you what is right if you will listen openly and with a willingness to love. Put rationalizations aside and face things squarely. One always must be open to divine guidance and redemption—always ready for grace. Yet at the same time, make an honest effort to get and keep your life straightened out. You know that if you try to cheat another, you succeed only in cheating yourself. If you lie to another, the lie will cloud your own mind. If you find yourself in a situation now that is born out of past misdeeds or bad motives, cut yourself free of the situation as quickly and as cleanly as possible, even if abruptly disentangling yourself from it appears to bring you a loss of some kind. It is better in the long run to be free of this kind of bondage at any cost and to seek instead the joy of open and honest relationships with others. Be truly free! Live lovingly and with your eye on the highest at all times and you will transcend the obstacles easily.

Be honest and face yourself. Do you hold an outright belief (or an indirect shadow of a "feeling") that any other race or nation or type of person is inferior to you, or that you may be essentially inferior to someone else? Don't believe it; cast off that ignorance like garbage. There are no lower and higher races, no less qualified nations, nor less likely sex or social status in which to know God.

People of every type, in every place, and in every time have reached God-realization. The Father comes to whomever prays earnestly and comes in whatever form the devotee worships Him. One form is just as real and divine as the other. If God appears to everyone who seeks, can there be anyone less worthy than another? The time to see Him is now, the place is here; you are the woman or the man to whom He seeks to reveal all Truth, just as every other woman or man is. Do not think about appearances. Turn to Him now with openness and love and see that all others also are turning to Him. Until you can behold God indwelling each one, you cannot see God "face to face" either in your meditation or in full manifestation in the world.

In the "dry times" you may think: But how can I maintain faith in people? So often they let me down! Keep attuned to the inner life; it is subtle, but always moving, growing, active, unfolding within each and all. The person who lashes out with a violent act, harsh word, a lie, or who does some foolishness may at the next moment see the light and express the Truth lovingly. Never accept falsehood or cruelty or weakness; be forever impatient with ignorance and selfishness. Treat these like bitter enemies, but forgive the woman, forgive the man. Open your heart to all with freeing love.

Has your heart been broken? Your heart of hearts cannot be broken. This is ever joyous and satisfied, loved and loving. Take a deep breath. Some are ready to give or receive more of the gift of love than others. Free them to their own good. Expand to give and receive more love in your own life each day. Be ready to love again and again.

Has someone slandered you? The Self of you cannot be slandered. Criticism and gossip simply will not stick to this Self; it laughs forgivingly at such talk.

Has someone robbed you of possessions? The Self of you is the very Source of all treasure. It is all that is worthwhile and good and enriching in the universe. The children may play in the king's treasure room; nothing can be taken out, therefore nothing can be stolen. The Self of you is the treasure room, and it cannot be robbed of its infinite good.

Has someone hurt you? Turn at once to the Healer of all. Be willing to be healed by His love on the outer and especially inwardly. Be willing to forgive the apparent wrongdoer of both kinds of hurt, and very soon, through His grace, the hurt and even the thought of the hurt will pass away.

Let love take over. Even when you experience hurt feelings because of another's actions, let love take over in your mind and heart. Think of a person who you have thought was against you. Can you forgive this seeming enemy with all-freeing love? Can you really love the person who appears to have broken your heart, or slandered you, or robbed you, or hurt you? If you cannot do this completely as yet, at least release the wish to retaliate or harm that person. Use mental or spoken denials of any wish to injure, and affirm instead pure and freeing love. Even if it takes some effort initially, persist and the trend of the mind will begin to change in a positive way. How much freer you will be! Whatever techniques you may want to use to help change your thinking and feeling, always continue to pray: *Lord, give me more love. Take away the obstacles in my mind, purify my heart, and let me receive and express only Your perfect love.*

Think of that perfect love. Think of divine forgiveness. Let your mind taste of this feeling. The old saying is wrong, after all—it is not revenge that is sweet, for revenge and resentment and regret are only bitterness. The freedom, release, and joy you seek is given freely in God's gift of love. Father-Mother God underlies your own nature and the nature of the seeming enemy as eternal sweetness and purity. God is omnipresent, dwelling within each without exception, and God is love. See how, through following these simple ideas, the mind goes from, Oh, this terrible enemy of mind, this rascal!—to, What liberating Truth—God is love!

Follow this trend of thinking and feeling. Follow the Self of you that is ever shining beneath the surface of thoughts, emotions, and experiences in life. This Self is leading you to much more Truth and joy than can be told in words. Therefore, follow the trend of forgiveness; follow the trend of love to the answers. Take a long moment now and follow the Self with all your mind and heart.

At last, the realization of love! This, then, is the "trick": expect good from others, yet manage not to be too distressed if they should fail to express absolute goodness. This requires great faith in the true nature of people. Otherwise, at the first failure of someone dear to you to live up to the ideal you envision for him, you would feel utterly hopeless and depressed. Do not let this happen. Keep your eye on the ideal—this has not changed. Pray for more perfect understanding, for greater love, and it will be granted. Love is God's grace. As you become a greater channel of His grace, your word, action, presence, and thoughts can save countless individuals from unnecessary suffering. Therefore, do not spend much time lamenting about the evil nature of many people. How easy it is to forget evil actions of the past when the light of Truth begins to dawn in the consciousness and starts to shine forth in the life of any person. Think of that Christ light, and love will come.

Do not worship people as people, but as the Divine in essence. Then you cannot be bound in worldly attachment to appearance or personality, but only to the Divine that you have worshiped and adored. Then you will be one in consciousness with divinity, free from mortal limitations.

You may think: I know that love for all beings and for all the world is part of the Christ consciousness toward which we all are unfolding. But how hard it is to love all people! What alternative is open to you? You may say, "Well, I will follow the path of wisdom, and as I attain greater and greater understanding, surely I will come to have Christlike love." Take the shortcut: simply love right now!

How tedious it would be to have to know every

tissue and thought of your beloved friend before you
could truly love that person. What grace, that only a
look, a word, a thought is exchanged, and instantly
there is love! The universe is like this; Truth is like
this. Infinite wisdom is the divine gift readily given to
the willing heart. Willingness to know all Truth, even
if it means giving up some cherished falsehoods, is
itself *love*. Be ever so willing, ever so loving, and be
one with all Truth. God answers your prayers for
more love with infinite speed. Only be willing to love
more, and you will see how quickly the heart is
opened!

Practice Exercise

Read the following three paragraphs, and then put
these pages aside and dwell on the ideas presented.

Become calm and peaceful. Sit with spine straight
and feel that the flow of life is easy, yet powerful
throughout your being. Relax your whole body, especially the hands. Let them be free of tension, as if to
give and receive a great and beautiful gift. Let your
hands rest open in your lap, and feel that divine love
is flowing forth from your open hands and returning
into them again in full, life-giving force in an eternal
cycle of love.

Think about these hands as the expressers of God's
love, as the channels of giving and receiving all good.
Think of your hands lovingly and see them whole and
beautiful in Spirit. They are open now, ready to give
and receive the gift of infinite love.

Let your hands be symbols of your open mind—ready to know all Truth from any source, ready to gather ideas from any person, and ready to express ideas to all who are ready to receive them. Let your open hands be symbols of your open heart—ready to forgive freely and to overflow with purifying love, ready to receive forgiveness freely and to be cleansed, healed, and uplifted by divine love. Know for yourself:

Through these hands divine love flows, inwardly and outwardly blessing myself and all the world.

Imagine the hands of holy persons in pictures you have seen. See them in your mind's eye as beautiful and gentle, always seeming to liberate, never to withhold a blessing.

Imagine angelic hands reaching out to uplift the human race—never grasping or clutching, full of love . . . releasing, releasing, releasing. Let these be your own hands.

Gently now, slip into a deep awareness of divine love. Close your eyes and let the free flow of eternal, everywhere present love be active in and through you.

Wherever healing is needed in your life, in the life of another, or in great masses of people, let divine healing love flow through you now and let this healing be complete. Extend the hands of healing to all the world. Free all to perfect healing. Know that divine love heals.

Wherever understanding is needed in your life, in

the life of another, or in great masses of people, let divine love flow forth through you now and let this understanding become full. Extend the hands of illumination to all the world. Free all to infinite wisdom. Know that divine love enlightens.

Wherever harmony is needed in your own life, in the life of another, or the lives of great masses of people, let divine, harmonizing love flow through you now and let the world be at peace. Extend the hands of peace to all the world. Free all to happiness and order. Know that divine love harmonizes and unifies.

Give thanks for the miracle of love that relates all beings to one another. Think of these things, keep notes in your Spiritual Diary. Give thanks that you and all people everywhere are unfolding.

In all that you do throughout this month, be mindful of your innate divine ability to bestow a blessing of healing, understanding, unifying, freeing love. The liberation of divine love can be conveyed in an actual touch, but more important, it is carried in the inner touch of mind and Spirit. This contact is the activation of unbounded creative power. Be receptive to miracles! Be open to miraculous change taking place in your own life this day, and be ready to let miracles happen to people all around you and throughout the universe, by your own hand. For God performs His perfect work through you.

Learning to Relate
A FOURTH STEP

Congratulations on your continued effort and growth toward greater love. It is good to be able to feel for mankind. The greatest souls have felt the most deeply for the world. How often in their life-times have they wept for the suffering of others! It is good to have the capacity to feel for and with others, and when you learn of someone's struggle, to be able to say like Walt Whitman, "I am the man, I suffer'd, I was there" (Song of Myself). Feel deeply, yet do not lose your sense of balance. Do not be dragged down by apparent suffering in the world, but instead set your heart on joy. This may seem difficult and

even callous to some persons, but it takes great
courage and love. You will not help the one who has
fallen into a ditch by getting down there too. Bring
joy and freedom into the world just as the great ones
throughout time have done: find joy and freedom
within yourself. It will spread through you, for this
activity cannot be stifled. Therefore, the work you
feel led to do for the sake of the world is primarily an
inward task. It centers in daily prayer and meditation. Give yourself over to God completely and love
will come of its own accord. The answers you seek
and the outer activity that ought to be done by you
will be unfolded for you. Set your heart on Him, for
through Him all good is accomplished and from Him
all love flows.

Lesson 4: The Cosmic Embrace

In the world, so often is heard the sound, "self,
self, self—embellish it!" Within his own psychophys-
ical makeup, man hears the mind and senses clamor,
"self, self, self—gratify me!" In metaphysical
studies, the emphasis is on realization and expression
of another Self beyond self, and even this can seem at
times to be only a slightly elevated selfishness. If you
feel the longing to shed selfishness like a skin that has
become too tight, be glad for that longing and follow
it through. As a concerned aspirant, you may say: "I
seek self-realization, but thousands all over this
world are starving, imprisoned, oppressed, suffering,
dying at this very moment. What does my own satis-

faction, either sensual or inspirational, really do for all these others? *What can I do*?"

By that very desire to help, you have begun. It is good now to think of the lives of those you revere most highly. Everyone who you may recognize in your own heart as "saint," or "God-incarnate," or "sage," or "great teacher" has been of twofold help and significance to the world. Each has helped certain individuals directly in the way of satisfying some material need. Think of all the ways in which these compassionate individuals have seen to it that others had food or shelter or healing. The example of such great people has inspired many others to continue in this vital charitable work. What a great boon this is to the world! But that work, however needed, is made so much more wonderful and precious to the world by the second and higher phase of these individuals' expression of love. They have helped certain blessed persons toward the all-important goal of God-realization. Through grace, they have signaled spiritual growth by a word, a look, a touch, a gesture, or by their presence alone. And these blessed individuals have carried this spiritual blessing to many others who in turn have blessed still more. And then, even those who have not enjoyed a direct relationship with such holy persons have been inspired by their example of spiritual life through the writings they have left or by the writings of their devotees. What a priceless gift! How much harder spiritual studies and practices would seem without these great souls to follow! Thinking about them and continually being humble and grateful for their guidance is a way to begin to truly appreciate the potential in this world. This is also a way to become a channel for their very personal blessing. See through them, and through all the changes and evolution in the world, the eternal presence of the Lord, and such love will grow in you as can transform the whole earth.

A picture of a saint in spiritual ecstacy stirs the mind. Somehow the onlooker from every kind of background feels inwardly a hint of that same joy. Every Truth student suffers inwardly to some degree because others are struggling and suffering. Yet even the joy of one small child adds light to the world. How much more light, then, the spiritual illumination of even one person gives to the world! Seek that illumination, that God-knowledge, and you will give the greatest gift to mankind.

Paul wrote, "faith apart from works is dead." If you accept the revelation, you will naturally be drawn to doing good and helpful things. Yet it is a common mistake to make service the goal, forgetting God-realization. Perform good works as a means to that end, ever beholding God at work through you and ever serving God through others. Think of it this way: good works apart from faith are dead. Through spiritual love, your faith becomes truly alive and whatever work you do in the world will be beneficial and life-giving. One who sets out with the ultimate goal of getting results by doing good for people, without having a spiritual ideal in mind, eventually will become frustrated and discouraged. Let your outer activities be prompted by sincere desire to reach and help others to reach conscious unity with God.

Then good works will be the natural expression of your high state of consciousness. When you help to provide food or shelter or healing for someone, it will have deeper and more lasting meaning than bread or a roof or some medicine; it will tend to suggest something higher and to bring with it a lasting blessing. You will not necessarily need to tack on a written or spoken message of Truth, for your gift will come from sincere love and love convinces, love teaches, love helps.

Love is easier than you think. You don't need to strain at it. Think of God, seek God, love God, and your life will be a blessing to all.

It is right that individuals who are coming into the awareness of Truth should feel impatient for a better world. What they may forget is that their own emergence as self-aware spiritual beings—even that very impatience and sense of urgency—is helping this world to be better in dramatic ways. This is not to say that charitable deeds such as feeding the hungry, educating the ignorant, and caring for the sick and confused are of no consequence in bettering the world. These are necessary acts, both for those who receive the aid and for those who give it, for all these things are true worship of God. However, without spiritual insight and impetus behind these acts, without *love*, the cure will not take, the results will not be lasting, the bandage simply will not stick.

The question may come: how does one *get* love? How is it that this all-important faculty is developed and expressed more fully? All possible answers may be reduced to two basic requirements: 1) Perform good works in the world; practice noninjury, truthfulness, purity, noncovetousness; and strive to improve the living conditions of as many people as possible. While in the midst of this activity, keep mindful of the real spiritual nature of each person and of the real spiritual nature of the act itself. 2) The way to keep this Spirit-mindedness is to habitually dwell in the presence of the Lord in prayer and meditation. Through daily spiritual practice the mind becomes ever more finely attuned to the divine nature moving in and through all, and you are strengthened against the upsets of appearances that would otherwise rob you of peace and happiness. The mind has made a habit of dwelling on the imperfections in life. In order to make the world better, it is necessary to change the habit of the mind so that it begins to dwell more and more on the divine perfection that waits in potential to be realized. Then you can help this potential to come forth.

The terrific fact is that the world is unfolding! This activity is intensified by your own conscious searching, and it radiates forth from you for the common good of all. This common good is God expressing; it is innate common knowing, "common sense," and it is real and far more significant than it may seem. On one level, it is what prompts most people to come in out of the rain. On another level, it is that common sensibility to spiritual truths. Be glad that it is present in everyone, even now coming into fullness.

Be glad you are living in the nation where you live, whatever nation it may be, for that "common sensibility" has instilled its government, customs, and mode of living with so much that is good, and more good is emerging. But look beyond that national love, accepting it and enjoying it for the great thing that it undoubtedly is, and reach to the love that is universal, encircling and embracing the whole world. Embrace the nation, but do not stop there; embrace the cosmos. You will find that the arms of your consciousness are expandable to hold all of it.

Can the consciousness of a human being expand? It may seem that the empirical limits of mankind are set, that we can only see so far and so well, or run such and such a distance at such and such a speed. And yet every day these limits are broken through. What does this suggest to you?

The mind and memory and reasoning capabilities of men and women have been demonstrated so dramatically in this era—in all eras—that it appears here too that any set limits can only be a passing notation along the way, scarcely set down before they are broken through and cast aside. When our "heart is in it" there is nothing we cannot do. What does this suggest to you?

In some instances, the human mind seems to have gone beyond what would ordinarily be called intelligence. The thoughts of men and women at various times and in various places on earth have gone up into a finer, loftier realm. Here reasoning becomes direct apprehension and feeling becomes love. Absolute knowledge is absolute love. Whenever you must honestly say, "There is something I do not love about that person," then actually there is something you do not *know* about that person . . . the Truth.

The whole Truth about him or her could signal only acceptance, understanding—love.

Here is the mystery: the Lord is one, yet many in His infinite aspects. You are one, yet many in your ability to experience all these aspects and be one in Spirit with everyone else in this universe—all expressions of God. The masses of people in the world with all their differences and personalities are telling you something. Can you hear the messages?

When your thinking begins to reveal that all are one in Spirit, and that things are really in harmony in spite of seeming confusion, your mind becomes infused with a great wisdom and peace about things and people. This is love blossoming. Give thanks, for your own sake and selflessly for the sake of the human race. Your own growth is brother and sister to the growth of others. Together you are a blessing to the world.

All Truth students come to the place in their experience when they feel like this: I have found the wonderful golden key to all of life's treasure. Surely this is just what people need and want, so I will gladly reveal it to them wherever I go!

Be careful. The motive here may be deceptive; it may still be a little attached, a little egotistic, for all its enthusiasm and high-soundingness. The story in Lesson 2 [p. 26] of the devotee who shouted a mantra to all who would hear, illustrates the purest love. But it is necessary to consider carefully whether in each case your motive is really the selfless seeking of liberation for all, or if it may be a subtle disguise for the desire to be the "answer man," when others really prefer to and need to find their own answers in their own way and at their own right moment. Be loving enough to free them to this wonderful experience.

It has been wisely taught by Indian masters, "Speak the truth, but never a harsh truth." To speak a harsh truth—one that comes too abruptly or is unwelcome—would be to violate the rule of harmlessness. At the same time, to speak other than the truth in order to flatter or placate someone would be to violate the rule of truthfulness and actually to harm. What is the answer? Love. Love so greatly that you would not wish to harm or mislead. How can you learn such love? Follow your spiritual ideal: think of God as perfect love. Emulate this ideal, follow this divine example.

Even enlightened teachers of the world have been shunned, tortured, and executed by those who heard their teachings. Therefore, when you do feel moved by the Christ within to share spiritual insight, do so no matter what and don't worry about the results. But don't be surprised if you get the "cold shoulder"! Be at peace and let the heart remain fixed on the spiritual ideal. If instead you receive praise, follow the example of the great teachers and keep your equanimity. Don't be cold, yet keep at peace with the heart ever centered in divine love. Take your rewards from the Lord.

There is no certain formula to use so that you will always speak words of Truth when it is appropriate and keep still when that is best, except this: follow Him, let Him lead you. Let Him express Truth in the most loving, freeing way through you, and trust Him

to keep you quiet at the right time, according to His
infinite wisdom and love. He is the Master, loving
Father, and also your Teacher. Let the mind and
heart be constantly open to His instruction. Then
when you find yourself teaching others—and you will
by your words, actions, and even by your silent
presence—be assured that it will always be in the
most helpful and loving way.

It is no good to rationalize that you would be a
much happier and more loving and spiritual person if
it were not for certain troublesome persons in your
life. The traits in others that can upset you the most
can also bring out the highest and best that is in you.
Instead of complaining or worrying about such obstacles, learn to meet challenges with love. Such
challenges in your life are urging you to expand your
understanding, your love, and your expression of
love. As you learn to give thanks even for the problems others seem to set for you, you will soon see that
you are better than you thought and that others are
better than you thought. Love will work this miracle!

Try to think more and more of Him at all times
and less of the human weaknesses in yourself or in
others. He is really there, through it all, guiding you
and all others to a higher understanding. Lovingly
and willingly open your heart to Him, and He will
carry you through. It will be easier for you to face
challenges and life will be much happier for you.

As you become more loving, you become more
humble. As you become more humble, you are of-
fended or hurt by others less and less. What good
sense it is to become more loving! Pray for love, and

see how much better and freer life becomes.

Keep working: be involved in charitable activities and support these works in every way you can. Also be involved with Truth teachings and help support this work in every way you can. Be loving and happy. Do not let yourself become depressed about the state of the world, no matter what outer things may indicate. Work with love and joyously keep your eye on the goal, for it is at hand. Never think that there is no help for the world, for there is. And never think that no one will help the world but you. You are not alone in this! By your love you are joining with countless others in uplifting the world.

Wherever life is lived, there you are. Wherever someone prays or chants the divine Name, or longs for God-realization, or hopes for a better life, there you are. Wherever someone dreams that the world can and shall be better, there you are!

Practice Exercise

Become still now and let the mind and body relax. Let the concerns of the day and the news of the world slip away from you. Let the feeling of love come to your mind and heart with the spontaneity of an embrace. Mother-Father God is everywhere, constantly embracing you with love. This is the love that reveals all, sustains all. This is the love that grants all prayers, this is the love that unites all. Think of this love as you inwardly affirm:

God embraces me now with love, love, love.

I am peaceful, I am fulfilled, and I am happy.

Give thanks as you take a long moment for this experience to flood your being. You feel it intensely
during this exercise; know that it is with you *always*.

Filled with the sense of divine nearness and love,
know that through your own conscious attunement
with Him, He embraces the world through you. Extend your arms mentally—physically too if that is
helpful to you—as if to let this embrace be expressed
as a blessing to the world. Become part of the love
that embraces all, uplifting and sustaining the
universe.

Affirm with gladness:

The love of God now embraces each and all.

The love of God now embraces each nation.

The love of God now embraces the whole earth.

*The love of God now embraces the cosmos, en-
folding all in peace, peace, peace, joy, joy, joy, love,
love, love!*

And together we give thanks!

More than you know, you are helping the world!
Keep notes of your thoughts and experiences this
month in your Spiritual Diary, and remember that
wherever you are, God is—present and near, embracing you in divine love. As you unfold, so does the
world!

Learning That God Is Law
A FIFTH STEP

Give thanks as you begin this lesson that there is a ceaseless and persistent law of unfoldment at work in your very being that leads you through this and through all experiences to greater understanding, greater joy, and greater expression of the Truth. The conscious search for Self-realization that you have undertaken brings continual proof of the mystery that your questionings do attract answers, that your seeking does bring revelation, for it is the law of your own unfolding consciousness that gives the answers you need and that brings the demonstrations in your life of the presence and the power of God.

As you continue in this conscious search, it becomes clearer that this is a universe of *Mind.* The power activated in the process called *thinking* is revealed to be the power that manifests and moves everything in the cosmos. It is seen that the waves of thoughts in consciousness bring direct results in experience. The process by which this happens may be called *law.* This law of the universe is Mind in action.

The law of the universe may be illustrated as a great wheel, ever-turning, endlessly whirling in a cycle of cause and effect. Yet the dedicated Truth student can go beyond the surface fatalistic definitions of this symbol and reach a truly positive and liberating realization. In every wheel there is a hub—a point of perfect stillness upon which all activity centers and depends. Without this center there is no movement, no turning of the wheel. Think of that central power of stillness and peace as you begin this phase of study and practice, and know that through the law of your own being, real understanding of God as law will come to you.

Lesson 1: The Waves

It is the nature of the mind to think, and nothing can still its continual procession of thoughts. Therefore, it would seem that law, the natural outpicturing of this incessant process, is inevitable, inescapable. It seems that there is no way to get outside of the eternal wheel of cause and effect, action and result, thought and outpicturing, because it is impossible to stop the mind.

Yet if you have been following these steps of lessons and exercises sincerely, the fear of this seeming "eternal trap" of law is beginning to leave you already. For you have surely had moments when the mind—though still ticking away thoughts—becomes so tranquil and uplifted and centered inwardly upon some idea of Truth that its action begins to go beyond the denseness of "ego" into the rarer atmosphere of the I AM. No matter if this experience is only a glimpse, a fleeting hint. You know that there is a realm of experience beyond the pleasure and pain of ordinary existence, and that this realm is accessible to you. You know that the treasure is there, and you are on the way to it.

This is a seeming mystery of the mind: that its very nature is relentless motion, evolution, change, flitting from one place to another, producing thought after thought after thought. At the same time, it is the very nature of the mind to indicate—at special moments—that all its power centers in a point of inner stillness where all wisdom and peace reside. This is also the mystery of law, for it seems to be the relentless pattern of action and reaction, yet by this very pattern we find indications that there is a changeless essence of pure Being from whence all power and force flow. Contemplate this mystery and it will reveal to you its deeper meanings.

God may be perceived as absolute Principle, unchanging law—the sum total and First Cause of the universe. Your own experiences and unfoldment will verify this perception and reveal the Truth that God is law. God may be perceived as all-loving Father-

Mother of the universe—personal and responsive and near. Your own experiences and unfoldment will verify this perception and reveal the Truth that God is love. Yet these two apparently contrasting perceptions of the same God (as love and as law) will only seem to contradict each other until that timeless moment in your own awareness when you realize in a way so clear as to transcend theology that God *is* law, and that this unchanging law is *love*. The mother does not cease to love her child; that love is the law of her being. Think of that love! All the words that might be used to describe absolute law also describe this divine love: unchanging, unhampered by appearances, undulled by time, inexorable, inevitable, inescapable, eternal. Such is the love of God.

Thinking in this way, perhaps you will soon begin to lose any hesitancy to accept the idea that God is law. Your loving Father-Mother is not really lost as you approach the study of this concept. The Lord has not been taken away from you, but is revealed in fuller glory. This Father-Mother is all the more real, all the more loving for you as your awareness expands in this way. The mother may still slap the child's hand as he reaches for the hot stove; through her law of love, she protects, she warns, and she teaches. The slap is prompted by love alone. The law is really grace—God's love in action. Even the apparently negative and painful experiences of life are God's love in action, however puzzling that can seem at times. Look up and see the Father-Mother God's face—how full of love! Then the difficulties and the obstacles of life are met so much more easily as you rest in the protection and guidance of God's embrace.

Give thanks for the law of the universe, ever working in all the intricacies of life experience. That law in action reveals the nature of divine love. Yes, God is absolute principle—but ever so watchful principle, ever so careful and loving. Through all things, this law is working, working, working, and the work is always the work of uplifting, liberating love.

Known or unknown, this law is the activity of your life on every level. You breathe with law, live with law, unfold with law. As you must have discovered by now, this law is revealed as the law of mind action whereby your thoughts are naturally outpictured. They attract or form into substance according to their character. What may be forgotten when this law of mind action is first used with conscious power is that the law is potent and continuous. That is, thought results in certain circumstances which tend to give rise to certain clusters of like thoughts, which in turn outpicture again, and all from that thought in an eternal cycle. If that original thought bears in it a tinge of error, such as jealousy or malice or pride, the cycle of circumstances and feelings that results will bear that taint and magnify it over and over. The outcome will be that sooner or later the "thinker" will begin to renounce or deny or purge his consciousness of this taint which has brought such undesirable influences into his life. Then as the relationship between thought and actual experience begins to occur to the thinker, he will see that his own mind is the source of all his misery and misfortune.

What power appears to lie dormant in this mind! What a force to guide and correct and perfect. For all the trouble that the mind seems to bring, remember always that it is your inner Teacher at work—actually bringing you through the experiences that tend to make you rely more and more on the Christ Mind in you.

It is not profitable to dwell upon the seemingly negative, destructive powers of the mind, for this same power may also be turned to unlimited expressions of divine reality. Somehow, through all the antics of this amazing mind, and in and through all the dazzle and the turmoil it may produce, its true nature may begin to peek out at you. For there is no pit of human suffering, however deep and black— nor is there a summit of worldly riches and honor— that does not suggest and teach and signify the true nature of humanity if only we will see the meaning.

When health, money, peace of mind, and happiness all seem to be going fast or have utterly vanished, the experiencer cries out, "Oh, I am being punished!" No, a fuller understanding of the law of the universe is yet to come. For the true meaning of it all is not to hurt, but to ultimately heal. The purpose is not to take everything away from you, but to finally give you all good. The idea is not to bewilder, but to present to you all Truth, to unfold to you all wisdom, to tell you all. The outcome is not to be grief and loneliness; no, the story is not over yet! The outcome is to be joy beyond all joy you have yet known and the embrace of infinite, divine love.

In these "low times" of life, practice prayer and

meditation faithfully. The strength you need to get through and the answers you need to have will surely come to you as you keep steadfastly on the path.

When, on the other hand, fortune is evident and life seems favorable, easy, and good—with a body strong and beautiful, a mind peaceful, and supply plentiful—take full advantage of these precious gifts. Use your resources fully to seek the meaning of life. Use your strength and energy to undertake great works. Use the blessing of a peaceful mind to meditate with and realize God. In these "high times" of life, practice prayer and meditation faithfully, for this is the grace of God in action. Through all experiences in life, gain equanimity; see that both the ups and downs are gifts of God through which you can reach ultimate joy and freedom. When some apparently bad thing happens, take it as a signal to seek God even more intensely than before, take this too as a special opportunity to seek and know God evermore clearly. Even the changes of life are within the law of the universe, God in action, for God is all in all.

The "lessons" of life keep on coming. They will not be stilled as long as the mind is not yet stilled. But if you can, begin to see even the hardest lessons as great gifts, for they are. In the overcoming of these challenges, in the "hanging on" to an ideal right through the experience, you make your way to the answer, the fulfillment, the greater Self that has been present all along. Begin to see the sweetest blessings of life as even sweeter than they appear, for all things suggest the nature of God.

There is change in life, for this *is* life! But there is also something changeless at the core of it all, and this is the Truth. Through the changes, hold fast to the changeless and you cannot ever be made to believe that you are losing out or that you are lost. The changes in your life happen according to the law of mind action, the constant "choosing" function of your mind through which you seek the experiences that will reveal to you, in your own perfect way and time, the spiritual nature of your being. What you call your mind is like the very tip of the iceberg. It is only what is just now "showing" of the infinite Christ Mind that is the true Self of you. This alone is changeless and real.

As you study the aspects of God as law, learn to keep watchful of the mind. At this point, do not try to make the mind thought-less in spiritual exercise, for the mind will trick you. It has been rightly said that trying to still the mind is as difficult as trying to still the wind itself. Yet as you contemplate the mind and its strength, see that the seeming power of the conscious mind and the subconscious mind (that great factory storehouse) is really the unlimited power of the Christ Mind at the center of your being. This Christ Mind can still the waves of the mind.

"And he awoke and rebuked the wind, and said to the sea, 'Peace! Be still!' And the wind ceased, and there was a great calm"—(Mark 4:39).

The Christ appears to be sleeping in this body, this vessel of life. It is awakened when you seek it and look to it for the answer, the guidance, the overcoming power. The Christ awakens in your consciousness to still the storm of thoughts as well as the waves of chaotic experiences in your world. " 'Peace! Be still!' And the wind ceased, and there was a great calm.'' How great is this calm!

Practice Exercise

As you begin this practice exercise, resolve to let the "waves" of the ups and downs of life experience subside so that the peace and balance of the inner life may come to the surface of the mind.

Get settled in your study place and slowly and purposefully relax the body. Take plenty of time to begin to feel physically comfortable and calm. Let the body become so completely balanced that you feel you could hold a small pan nearly filled with water on your lap between your hands without sloshing or spilling any of the water. Close your eyes for a moment and practice this peaceful and relaxed balance, as if you were actually holding this pan of water.

Now that the body is calm and peaceful, the mind is naturally more calm and peaceful too. Think that the mind is like this same pan of water. Let the mind become as calm as the water, so totally still that light reflected upon it would shine forth clear and unbroken from the surface. Think that the Christ light is shining onto the surface of your mind right now. The waves of distracting thoughts become stilled and the Christ light shines clear and bright. You are filled with a sense of enlightened peace, and the knowledge that all is well now soothes and renews you.

If any unwanted thoughts should interrupt your peaceful contemplation, listen for the gentle command to the waves of the mind from the inner Christ Mind: "Peace! Be still!" Feel the great calm filling your being now as you are enfolded with the tranquillity of Christ.

Return each day this month to your place of study and practice this simple exercise. Know that you are a spiritual being, renewed and uplifted by the Christ Mind in you. As you write of your experiences and insights in your personal Spiritual Diary during this month, you will begin to see a new "you" emerging—a more peaceful and balanced "you." Keep an open and thankful attitude as you meet all the events of life, for you are continually unfolding in spiritual awareness and power. Recognize that God is active within and around you as the great law of the universe; and be happy, for through God's love in action, you are coming into a fuller and freer life.

Learning That God Is Law
A SIXTH STEP

Sooner or later each of us will come to the realization that she or he must learn to work with law. All life is growth, unfoldment. Therefore, strive to make this growth as smooth and painless as possible through a loving recognition that God is active in and through everything that takes place. God as law is manifest as all natural physical law that is observed in this universe, and He is active also as unseen law that is always in operation everywhere.

Recognize the possibility that divine law is the reason behind everything that happens to you—even the occurrences you may consider trivial and meaningless. Then let your mind follow after this possibility toward the meanings of many things in your life that may be baffling, whether they have come about as what looks like extreme good fortune or apparently unwarranted misfortune. Take these questions with you into the silence and see what answers you can receive from the Christ Mind.

You will begin to see that growth is taking place through these events—your own growth as well as the growth of others—toward the common goal of Self-realization. Perhaps you will even begin to marvel at it all, for the process of unfoldment that is taking place within and around you is taking place throughout the cosmos. You might perceive this process like the opening of the petals of a great universal lotus flower, or like the birth of a gigantic, radiant star system. When the thought of this great unfoldment makes you catch your breath and feel the beginnings of an overwhelming happiness, you are ready to know for yourself that God is law and to know the fullness and joy of this wisdom.

Lesson 2: First Things First

The universe is enfolded and ordered and embraced in a law of continual corrective, directive, delivering, infinite Principle. When you begin to sense this activity as real and immediate in your life and affairs, you will surely feel a new strength. You can undertake the challenges and you can meet the real issues of life with triumph, for this is God's will for you and it is the fulfillment of the law of your being.

Accept one thing: the nature of this world is change. By becoming attuned to divine law, you cannot preserve just certain desired outer conditions indefinitely; this is not the nature of spiritual mastery and dominion. What does happen is that you become so attuned to the *changeless* that the outer changes continually taking place will begin to seem to be a kind of divine "play." Now you can begin to feel really at one with the continual flow of unfoldment that is inexorably happening . . . always and always. You can welcome the flow of active and progressive life, for you can begin to feel the "fun" of it!

When you start to make these ideas your own, try saying to yourself:

I recognize that life has a message for me, and I go forward now to receive this message of Truth and to demonstrate in wonderful ways the strength, wisdom, and love of God-with-me.

Remember, through every "test" of life, God-with-you is present, mighty in your midst, and ready to help and teach you. He is nearer than you had thought, and far more powerful and loving.

Through the ages, people have admired heroes and heroines—persons who have emerged victoriously through great trials. People perceive that these victorious ones have proved a potential that all persons share. But how could that great potential be revealed except through challenge? The greater the obstacle, the greater the strength required to overcome it. Then it is with openness and even with joy that life's natural challenges should be acknowledged and accepted, for through them the fineness of spiritual potential is revealed.

Legendary heroes and heroines have often been endowed with some special talisman or secret formula that helped them to overcome tremendous odds. But there is no rabbit's foot so lucky, no flying carpet so quick, and no magic word so potent as the Truth, the light that shines within you at this moment. In the stories, the talisman is sometimes lost or stolen, or the magic word is temporarily forgotten. But real life is better than a story, for the "magic" that is the Self of you cannot ever be lost or stolen. (You have no "evil enemy," except your own error thoughts!) And the Self will not be forgotten either—it is as if it keeps leaving "messages" all around, little "notes" by way of people and events that come along with something to say to you in a subtle way about the presence and transcendent power of the Self. This is God as active law seeking to reveal, through everything, your true nature. Are you getting the message?

The "note" may come as a health challenge. God-with-you as the law of your own unfoldment is telling you: "Think of Me—see Me in this. I am your strength and wholeness—I AM!"

The "message" may come as an apparent lack of supply. God-with-you working as the law of your unfoldment is saying: "Think of Me—see Me in this. I am your abundant supply—I AM!"

In your relationships with others, in the books that come into your hands, in the ideas that come to your mind, God-with-you is ever leading, teaching, hinting: "Think of Me—see Me in this. I AM the Way and the Truth and the Life!"

Bless the means by which the message of Truth comes to you. Keep first things first: it is the new understanding, the greater love, the firsthand experience of the presence and power of God that is essential in life. However you get this message, praise God!

Consider what it really means to put first things first in life. Try to get at the beginning in your concept of life. Think of creation; what comes first? Is it not First Cause, the Creator, God? Is this not what must always come first in a true understanding of life? Perhaps here is the answer to all your questions, ultimately, and the way to see how God as law is now at work in your life. See the law in operation through the workings of your own mind: first comes a thought, then follows the result that is the natural outpicturing of that thought, and clusters of related thoughts follow that also become manifest. What is the purpose of this marvelous law of mind action? It is ever to instruct, to guide, to free. For when you are in the middle of the deepest despair, the worst problem, you will come to wonder: My God, what is happening to me? Why? What does it mean? And, when you seem to be having some unexplained "good luck" or when a special feeling of grace and well-being and sheer pleasure comes over your mind unexpectedly, like a too-early springtime, you may wonder: My God, what is happening to me? Why? What does it mean? See how in both kinds of experience the Self is leaving you "notes" again? See how the mind will tend to put first things first in the final analysis? What is the message from the Christ phase of your mind? Has the experience at hand brought you to readiness to receive a higher meaning, to where you must have a more complete answer than the old answers you had settled for before?

So many questions, and they can only be answered by you in the aloneness of your own seeking and through the uniqueness of your own experiences. You can see now how impossible it is to grow for another, or even to pretend to know what God means to reveal to someone else through a certain set of experiences. Each must find the answers for himself. Give no judgments; only the purest, most freeing love. Never turn up your nose at another person; the outer appearance may seem low and miserable and even disgusting to your ego-self. But do you know how near another person may be to a dramatic breakthrough in God-realization? Can you tell? It may be that the person you feel inclined to condemn or categorize too abruptly is but a hairbreadth from sainthood, or has already reached it. Don't fall into the pit of pride; use the bridge of love and accept each and every one as a fellow companion on this journey toward conscious unity with God. It may even be that someone's appearance of being in a terrible "fix" in life is all part of God's "play" to teach you. Let judgments go. They will only bind you tighter and make your own lessons harder. Say with humility and trust, "He is the Teacher; I am the student." The outcome of this attitude will be that His teachings of love and liberation will come to you ever so much more easily, and you will learn—answers of infinite blessings and light.

The goal of life is not to discover some gimmick whereby you can eliminate all of the waves of life's experiences and have it all smooth sailing. How dull that would be! Sooner or later you would want to be free of such an existence and to seek a chance to wrestle a little with life. The smoother and straighter life appears, perhaps the more "stuck in the mud" it really is; if so, the greater the lesson will be that is sure to come along and upset the boat. Give thanks even for the upset, for it is teaching you eternal things and breaking down immense barriers of bondage for you.

The goal is to eliminate the unnecessary suffering in life, so that you may boldly take on the good, freeing, cleansing lessons through which real heroism blooms. A true heroine is not someone who endures a willfully self-inflicted wound or obstacle. Do not punish yourself or torture yourself mentally or physically, seeking to answer the law expediently in that way. This only builds the ego, the prison house, the selfish will, instead of aiding a loving surrender to the freedom and wisdom of divine will. To make a good beginning in the understanding and attainment of conscious oneness with universal law, and to be able to accept all its workings with love and thankfulness, it is necessary to let the personal will be surrendered to divine will. You will lose nothing and gain everything good, as you will see.

No matter what happens to you and whatever you do, don't lose heart. You are never alone, for the

Christ is with you. Many Truth students who have
for a long time been seeking to apply the law of mind
action positively through loving, Truth-filled
thoughts and words, may have some tragedy befall
them in outer life. Look to the heart of things; however, keep first things first. Is there not still that place
of bliss and peace within? That cannot be lost or
ruined regardless of outer circumstance. That alone
is real and satisfying. Hold onto God and the answer,
the fuller life, the higher outcome will emerge
without fail. The divine message is still: "Think of
Me—see Me in this, for I AM with you always!"

Therefore, take a positive attitude in everything.
Use the cleansing power of denial against the real
"enemies" of life—false and limiting habits of thinking and feeling. Use positive affirmation to hold to
the real and changeless good that underlies all things.
The tools of denial and affirmation are indeed gifts
of Spirit, for through them you can truly stride over
even the biggest obstacles. Through these methods,
seek always to keep first things first. Keep this
positive, full-of-life outlook, and you will reap satisfying and constructive results from every experience.

Practice Exercise

As you prepare for this practice exercise, resolve to
get at the beginning of things in your consciousness.
Become outwardly still and relaxed, inwardly attuned
to the eternal messages of Spirit. Pause after this
paragraph and let the law of your own unfoldment

work freely, leading you through this exercise and through all the experiences of your life to new peace and wisdom.

Deny outer circumstances any power over you. Think of the very challenges you are meeting now in life; face them without fear. Try using this statement of denial, or one like it:

I deny that this situation has any negative influence on my soul growth; this cannot bind me; this cannot hold me in a state of suffering and confusion.

Take a deep breath now and know that through the law of mind action, what you have believed and declared is so.

Now take the second step: affirm your spiritual strength to overcome appearances and your divine birthright of freedom and victory with these statements, or statements like them that have special power for you:

I affirm the transcendent nature of the Self of my being. Through God-with-me I now am strong, I now am wise, I now am loving, I now am free. I open my mind and heart to the divine message that the Christ Mind has for me.

Endeavor to feel that you are wholeheartedly releasing yourself and your life to the outworking of divine law. Take several deep breaths; feel free and happy, for through the law of mind action, what you have believed and declared is so.

During this month, think of these statements taken from the lesson material; get at the Truth of them and let the Christ phase of your mind teach you the meanings you seek in life:

"All life is growth, unfoldment."

"Divine law is the reason behind everything that happens."

"The universe is enfolded and ordered and embraced in a law of continual corrective, directive, delivering, infinite Principle."

"I recognize that life has a message for me, and I go forward now to receive that message of Truth and to demonstrate in wonderful ways the strength, wisdom, and love of God-with-me."

"He is the Teacher, I am the student."

Through all the marvelous changes in life, know that God is telling you: "Think of Me—see Me in this. I AM the Way and the Truth and the Life! Think of Me—see Me in this, for I AM with you always!"

Be sure to add to your Spiritual Diary the unique and divine messages you are receiving.

Keep a positive attitude. Keep God first in your mind. Recognize that you are unfolding, unfolding, unfolding, like the thousand-petaled lotus, ever opening from your God-center of perfect eternal light. Give thanks with all your being that this Truth is so.

Learning That God Is Law
A SEVENTH STEP

God is that universal principle of good with which
you have been seeking to become consciously at one.
Do not think of this universal principle of good as
some distant orbiting force, far away as the rings of
Saturn. Think how close the law of gravity is to you
right now. Does gravity not affect this body in every
single part? Does the same law of gravity not affect
you all of your life? Know that the universal principle
of good is far closer, more affecting than any observ-
able physical law. Think of this closeness, this all-
encompassing nature. Is this not like an embrace?
Think of the embrace of the divine Parent—how

loving, how gentle, how caring. When you can recognize the law of the universe as all-good, and when you are altogether in harmony with this universal principle of good, then how comforting and uplifting you find this embrace!

Lesson 3: Father-Mother

All things in the universe are under the rule of the one great Mind—and the law of this Mind action is absolute love. Negative appearances are the apparent results of mistaken identity on the part of individuals who make the error in thought that there is mind other than God-Mind, or that evil exists as an absolute reality in the world. These conditions are only seeming and in the mistake there seems to be suffering. Give the mystery of mind over to Father-Mother God, and the answer will be given to you through grace—God's law of responding, all-knowing love in dynamic action.

What is it that you feel you need? Is it greater purity? Let God-Law be active in you now to purify and sanctify. Do you seek peace in the world, in your family, in your own mind and heart? Let God-Law be active in and through you now as a peace-giving, harmonizing presence. Do you need money or healing? Let God-Law be active in and through you now as substance and wholeness. Do you long for true wisdom? Let God-Law be active in you now as enlightening love, for He is the answer to it all. Do you look for justice and order in your affairs? Let God-

Law be active in and through you now as perfect justice and divine order in everything. Do you want power to overcome some obstacle that you see before you? Let God-Law be active in you now as infinite power for good. Do you ask for more love? Let God-Law be active in you now, and you will experience love, you will attract love, you will express love.

Here is the Truth: If you can always hold to the awareness of God as personal and all-loving and all-wise, you will be in harmony with law. This is practicing the presence of God in all things, and this allows you to remain a constant inlet and outlet for the universal principle of all good. Let your mind dwell consciously in God-Mind—think of God. There is no other way to realize law and, in fact, it is easiest for people to think constantly of something or someone that is beloved. Therefore, develop love for God—through prayer and meditation, through denial and affirmation, through any and all means that appeal to your nature. Let God be personal to you so that you may love Him more. You need only love God—that is the fulfillment of the law.

Nothing purifies the mind like perfect love. When the mind is pure its action is pure; when the action of the mind (thoughts and feelings) is pure the natural results that outpicture are always pure and good. This law is love.

Jesus, the great Master and the embodiment of love in the world, taught that the seeker of God must become like a little child. Therefore, endeavor to become guileless, open, loving as a small child. Then spiritual experience will have real meaning and transforming power for you.

Perhaps you have heard a song called "Scarlet Ribbons." Supposedly, the song is in the form of a story told by a loving parent who has overheard his child praying a simple prayer for some pretty scarlet ribbons. The parent at once believes that if the child's prayer is to be granted, the parent himself must go out and get some scarlet ribbons for the child before the child awakens the next morning. He hurries out into the town, but it is late and all the stores are closed. At last he comes home brokenhearted, certain that the child will be disappointed. But when he happens to look into the child's room, he sees that some scarlet ribbons have somehow already been placed there, and he is amazed. Relinquish the anxiety of the adult in the story, and enter into the nature of the child.

There is a child within everyone who trusts in the loving, all-providing nature of God. But the grown-up ego-self still tries to do everything the hard way. It is often better not to try to work out the puzzle of the law of cause and effect in the outer, but to trust completely in the loving Father-Mother to bring forth the answer that is needed.

This kind of guilelessness is the aim in spiritual life; and yet in the pursuit of God-realization, how many complex and intellectual explanations are built up about God, universal law, infinite Principle! It is exceedingly difficult to be totally free of at least some degree of intellectual pride about these fine metaphysical systems. This pride is a great obstacle. That is not to say that metaphysics and careful, scientific definitions about the nature of God may not be true and helpful. This way is valuable, but the aim of simplicity and childlike receptivity to God must not be forgotten, and it is most easily followed through devotion.

The sincere and honest Truth student may truly state, *God is infinite, omnipresent, omniscient, omnipotent principle, unchanging and eternal.* This is Truth. But when the same individual finds himself "up against" what appears to be the bitter side of this law of cause and effect, he may then cry out, "Father God, please help me!" The student has not slipped backward—there is only progress on this path, always a fuller realization. The student has recognized in a real and personal way that God and God alone is the source of his help. This realization is a great breakthrough in the spiritual life. One begins to see how the many facets of experience forever tend to reveal the many facets of God. He is always teaching, guiding, demonstrating His limitlessness, and revealing your limitless potential as well.

Never look down upon someone who holds to a very simple concept of God as Mother or Father, believing that this way of thinking must eventually be outgrown in favor of a finer, loftier, more abstract concept. Do not be enslaved by such limited judgments. The Lord is all these things—one and the same. Do not be afraid to put metaphysics aside for a time in your search for God-realization. Do not be afraid to turn and become "like a child" no matter how far along in this search you have traveled.

Without the guilelessness of a child, you cannot enjoy this world, much less God-realization. Without guilelessness, the shell of the ego is too hard, the door of the mind too tightly guarded by thoughts of "I" and "mine" to let in the bliss of God.

Pray earnestly:

Father-Mother God, You have made this universe and all that is in it. You are the Creator and the Sustainer of it all. Teach me, reveal Yourself to me!

Nothing can be achieved in worldly life without the earnest desire to accomplish it. In the spiritual life as well, nothing can be achieved without longing. Then, when events in life cause you to develop more longing for the Truth, give thanks, for that longing will be satisfied.

Another way to see the constructiveness of the personification of law as Mother-Father or Father-Mother is to realize that so long as the seeker thinks continually of God as abstract Principle only, he may begin to feel separate from the loving nature of God, and to dwell on the importance of his own responsibility and initiative in this universe of law to such an extent that he may feel this personal responsibility as a great burden. He may begin to worry and worry so much about the effects of his every thought, word, and action that he forgets grace. Grace is God's love in action, and since God is love and God is law, then the law is love and love is the law. Dwelling too much on the personal self will build the ego-sense and hold the individual back from a full realization of the true nature of law. Some students who sense this kind of bondage even temporarily, stop using affirmations that begin with the words *I am,* and use instead only statements that begin, *He is,* or *Father-Mother God is,* or *Thou art,* stressing the loving, all-encompassing, personal aspect of God. The thought is to change the emphasis from "I" (which may tend to be ego-linked) to "It is He," God beyond all limitation of personality.

In the Spirit, dedicate "good" luck to Father-Mother God. It is from God, it is God's expression in your life, God's gift to you. Do not think of the good things and pleasant experiences in life as having been strictly earned by you because of your own good works and right thinking. Instead, see God as the one Source of all good and mentally dedicate all that you have to Him, giving thanks continually for His blessings. If you think that you are the source of anything in life, the ego will gain strength and you will have to wrestle with it.

You may think that by letting selfishness, anger, or greed rule you, you can somehow elude the natural consequences, but these errors are tied to you. They are like a balloon tied to your clothing by a string; you may think they are gone, but the breeze changes direction, or you turn around, and there they are. You must deal with them all in time. Error thinking—called sin—brings forth its own result. If you put your hand into the flame, you will be burned. Such is the nature of things on the limited, sense-bound level. But there is a transcending law, and in this law is freedom. Seek this with all your mind and heart, for this alone can free you. Open your heart to

God now—this is what the law is telling you—and He will make you free.

A man becomes restless in a low-paying and unfulfilling job; he becomes so restless that he seeks something that is better for him. In the same way, a person will sometimes feel restless with a limited understanding and expression in life and seek the Truth with new zeal. The outer experiences that made him restless are good, for they have helped him to feel the longing for a better way. That longing is a call to the Lord, which by the very law of His Being, He cannot fail to answer.

God acting as personal Lord cannot resist your longing. Only pray guilelessly, without pride or egotism, with genuine longing, and this prayer will have special power. Remember always that God is your *very own*, and do not hesitate to approach Him.

Don't give any thought to what blessings you may feel you have earned in life or to what great burden of sin you think you have created for yourself. Do not think of law in this way, for that will keep you bound. Think of God as your loving Father-Mother.

Realizing the nature of the Father-Mother's love, one feels much less urgency about the gratification of sense pleasures, or about the gaining of any mental or occult powers, or about the obtaining of worldly possessions. One feels a natural contentment from this love alone. This joy is evidence that conscious harmony with God—divine law—is the only permanent and real answer to the apparent evils and sufferings of this world. Like a trusting child, hold no doubt about the love and giving nature of your

Father-Mother God. Remember always that God is your very own. Come to God with the confidence and openness of a child.

In the assurance of this Presence with you, declare:

I deny that I inherit sickness, sense-bondage, lack, ignorance, or any imperfect condition; for through divine law in action, my Father-Mother God gives me wholeness, freedom, abundance, wisdom, and joy. I give up the past—it is worn-out; and with thanksgiving I claim God's gift now with all my heart.

Beloved, this gift is yours.

Practice Exercise

As you become still and relaxed, become attuned to the omnipresent loving activity of God. Open your hands on your lap or at your sides, open your mind to receive infinite wisdom and bliss, and open your heart to receive the inflow of divine love. Become like a small child—even feel that you have grown smaller in size. Feel that you are without guile, without selfishness, without pretense. Let your whole being be an open channel to the infilling of love. No matter what challenges you are meeting in your outer life, place all questions and problems lovingly in God's hands. Make of your heart a prayer; make of your mind a prayer; make of your body a prayer. Use prayer statements like the following and progress to sincere and simple words that come from the depths of your own heart. First, close your eyes for a moment and feel that you are becoming childlike in innocence and receptivity. Feel that the loving Father-Mother God is ever so near to you, listening and responding to the longing of your heart, for that is true.

Let your mind follow these words, let your heart enter into the feeling they express, and then let the genuine feelings from your heart be expressed in your own personal prayers. Begin by thinking of these words, sanctifying them into true prayer through your sincere longing and love.

Father-Mother God, let this body be in harmony with Your law of perfect life. Rest like a child in the arms of the Lord, and know that this prayer is answered.

Father-Mother God, let my life be in harmony with Your law of continual unfoldment. Rest like a child in the arms of the Lord, and know that this prayer is answered.

Father-Mother God, let my material supply be in harmony with Your law of infinite abundance. Rest like a child in the arms of the Lord, and know that this prayer is answered.

Father-Mother God, let my mind be in harmony with Your law of absolute wisdom and peace. Rest like a child in the arms of the Lord, and know that this prayer is answered.

Father-Mother God, let me be in harmony with Your law of divine love. Rest like a child in the arms of the Lord, and know that this prayer is answered.

Father-Mother God, let me be in harmony with You. Rest like a child in the arms of the Lord, and know that this prayer is answered.

Now enter wholly into the attitude of fulfilled love. Rest in this love, knowing that it is the fulfillment of the law in your life.

Write your personal prayer statements in your Spiritual Diary; use them during this month in the quietness of your meditation time, and keep them silently in mind as often as possible. Know with each heartfelt prayer that the answer is already there, for this is the loving nature of God-Law.

Keep a feeling of trust and joy, and always give thanks, for by the unfailing action of universal law, you are ever and ever unfolding into infinite bliss and fulfillment.

Learning That God Is Law
AN EIGHTH STEP

You know that your body moves most gracefully and easily when you feel in harmony; it is then in a kind of physical rhythm that seems natural, in tune with your real beingness. The mind is most efficient in problem-solving and understanding the true nature of things when it is calm, centered in the still wisdom that is the underlying power of the mind. And the universe works most harmoniously and peacefully whenever there is conscious attunement to that essence that transcends appearances. Draw from these things the concept that the nature of God—the nature of law—is completely beyond the outer, although the divine presence is revealed through this world of effects.

Contemplate the difference between action and rest. In action, some power is demonstrated; in rest, all power is latent, complete, in repose. Action is the use of power, not power itself. This huge universe, with all its many phases and whirling worlds and ceaseless motion, is as but a gesture of God. His power is in part revealed through the created universe, yet there is infinite power remaining unseen in this outer world. The wonder is, however, that you can become consciously at one with this omnipotent Presence, this ocean of bliss. You can know God.

Lesson 4: The Ocean

It has been taught that God is law, that God is also love, and that love in action (grace) is the fulfillment of the law (God revealed in the world, yet beyond all form). Therefore, the student rightly draws the conclusion that grace (the free gift of spiritual freedom) is attained by letting the heart and mind become open to God through love. Do not worry if it feels impossible to love God without form or attribute, to love God as law in the absolute sense. He cannot be limited, really, not even by the worship of God with attributes such as, love, wisdom, power, and peace. A wise teacher has taught that God is like an iceberg: the iceberg appears to be different from the ocean, yet in reality it is of the same substance. God assumes form and attribute so that mankind can love Him more easily, and through that love come to know Him. The warmth of the growing love of the devotee melts the iceberg into the ocean, and the devotee comes to know God as limitless. Therefore, simply love God in whatever way He seems closest, most real to you. His law is to be revealed to you according to your nature and your desire. He cannot be known through words—*experience Him.*

God is experienced through love. Love has been defined as that which unites, binds, holds together everything in the universe. This definition implies that love has the nature of law in that it is constant, unbreakable—a "system," or principle. God is love and He is also the activity of loving. Whenever you express love, you are in accord with the activity of law, which is love purified. You cannot separate love from God any more than the warmth and light and ability to burn can be separated from fire, for the law of His Being is love itself.

The true nature of God as law is realized not through merit, but through grace—love. No one really feels he has earned love, for love from any source is felt as a free gift, as grace. This grace is felt as love received from parents, teachers, friends, even from that Christ self that is ever guiding and teaching you through all life's experiences. Grace is attunement with law in its perfect working. Physically, this grace is felt as a biological harmony, as well-being, balance. It is the sense that life is good just because it is life; that it is great to be alive. Mentally, this grace is felt as being in tune with one's own ideals in life. It is peace of mind, equanimity, joy—the joy of understanding, of perceiving through the wondrous instrument of mind. Spiritually, this grace is felt as the growing awareness that in all things, "not I, but Thou." This is the same law, the same grace operant on all levels at one and the same time. When grace is felt to be in activity, the flow of life freely follows the underlying current of Spirit, which leads always to freedom.

The essence of the law is beyond the realm of effects, although its activity is perceived there. Therefore, forget results and think of pure love, pure Being, as much as possible. Then you will be all the more in tune with the law, which is pure love, pure Being. With the mind attuned to the underlying harmony, the underlying current, you find that you meet challenges in life much more easily. The flowing stream appears to yield to obstructions in its path, passing on quickly around them. In this way, it steadily wears down the rough edges of the obstructions and finally reduces them to nothing, and the stream flows on unimpeded. Ultimately, the seeming obstacles also join the flow of the current, and all are one in harmony.

Bigotry, selfishness, ignorance, stubbornness, and prejudice will fall away from the personality of the one who seeks God sincerely, looking always for evidence of His presence, His nature as law acting through all people and events in the world. What is to be hated or feared? There is a divine lesson, a swift undercurrent guiding and lifting each and all toward the ocean of wisdom.

The paradox is that God, in essence beyond

change, even beyond activity, moves as a current of Spirit in creation. In reality, God (Law) is beyond all change, even beyond all activity. God is reality—fulfilled, perfect, complete already, now, and wanting nothing. Therefore, He is beyond action or working, for all is already perfect in God. Only in appearance is there less than perfection. On this level, God appears to act in order to bring about the realization of the perfection already attained in Spirit. Remember the story of the king who dreamed that he was a beggar and awoke from that delusion to find that he had been a king all along? The goal is to awake from the dream to the spiritual reality.

Hold the idea before your mind for testing, that the Godhead—God as pure Being—exists above and beyond all attributes, forms, and manifestations; these are but a pressing out of Him Who remains unchanging at the ground of all. See whether your mind can touch the idea somehow, and whether the idea has not been at the back of your mind always. Such an idea tends to make intellectual quibbling become small and eventually be worn down to nothing. It leaves in its wake only a peace and sureness about things that no ordinary reasoning can give.

There is a part of you that is one with this Truth. The very Christ self of you is beyond all outer happenings around you. You do not perceive this Self as cold, even though it is untouched by pain, suffering, sadness, birth, age, death, decay. God is of that same nature: not cold, yet apart from all appearance, still working as inexorable Principle toward the unfoldment of the universe. Just as God is law, that God-self of you is the law of your own being. It is working silently, never resting (although it is, in essence, perfect peace and perfect rest), ever leading you toward spiritual freedom.

The God-self of you is hinting that at-one-ment with divine law holds for you all conceivable treasure and benefits. The individual who is experiencing a growing sense of conscious oneness with God as law is making the transition from the constant feeling that he is laboring against something in life—trying to swim upstream—to the sureness that he is flowing with the current of all good. From struggle to the ease of sureness and peace, this is the change that is taking place.

Human conceptions of law arising out of finite mind are at best limited—second best to divine law. The ideal way to live, therefore, would be to perceive directly and to become consciously at one with divine law. Then the whole being is in tune with perfect law and cannot transgress that with which it is one. This pure perception can only be received by the pure mind. And the mind becomes pure through contemplation of Truth and meditation on God. This is the most direct way to bring about order in this manifest plane. It begins with each individual; it begins with you.

This is not to say that human law should be ignored because it is necessarily limited. The goal is selflessness and enlightened selfhood. Is it not true that violation of man's law most often comes through the doer's self-seeking? Follow human law in reverence to the more perfect divine law, which is, even through the imperfect human law, seeking to be revealed to mankind.

Human law appears to be only so many volumes of words in print, filling many libraries. Yet when someone transgresses this law or urgently needs the protection of the law, the officers of the law should be very quickly at hand to enforce the law for the correction and/or protection of all concerned. God as law can seem a dead thing—a collection of proverbs from scriptures and theological treatises, an abstract concept removed from the real world. Yet whenever divine law is ignored, how quickly and effectively its enforcement works.

It is not possible to "have" the law, that is, to "use" it for personal satisfaction in life—this body, these possessions, these friends and relatives, this money, this diploma, these children—for all life belongs to the Lord, the law of the universe, and not to any finite being. You do not have the law, the law has you. A swimmer in the ocean does not possess the ocean, but rolls with its waves and feels its vastness. Learn to feel with faith and openness, "not I, but Thou," in all your actions in life and you will know the wonder and freedom of divine law in action.

One might very well think, But how is it freedom for me, if I must give up all my own desires and personal will, submitting all to God? This question is secretly asked by everyone at some time, and it seems always to come with a sense of desperation, ego-self dependence, fear of losing the personal identity. And this question only comes when the seeker has lost touch momentarily with the Truth that God is the source of all power, all joy, all freedom. Conscious separation from this Source is not freedom, but bondage and limitation. God is not dry, but joy, more full and sweet than any other you have known. What you have to lose are only the negative, restricting aspects of your personality; what you have to gain is the strengthening of that spiritual identity that is ever beautiful, pure, perfect, and eternal. You can't drown in this sea of immortality, but only find a new vastness, a new liberation. Keep following your inner perception that the study of Truth is carrying you onward to greater happiness, and let the minor fears and misgivings be swept away.

As you lose the struggle for personal gain in your work, or in the performance of any act whatsoever, your concentration is naturally intensified since it is freed of attachments and distractions. Then the work that you do and the acts you perform will take on a fineness that is striven for in all art. No matter how humble the work is, or how simple the act, it will be beautiful and good.

The choices you have to make in life become clearer, the way easier in this sense, the more the mind is attuned to God. Then do not forget the personal aspect of God, even though you are consciously dealing with God as principle, for the personal aspect of God as parent, friend, teacher, companion, is ever so easy to love and thus easy to keep in mind. When the mind dwells in God, law does its perfect work in and through you.

The mind is apparently made up of changing phases, yet derives all of its power from the underlying changeless One. God is apparently a continual display of changing manifestations, moods, and aspects; but is also that underlying changeless One. The water of the ocean is the same in essence, whether it is moving or still. The waves are only on the surface—the ocean of pure Being remains undisturbed. Beneath the mind of man, this One exists. Even underlying all action and power attributed by human mind to Mind, is that which is beyond all description. He will not fit into any definition!

This is not just because He is greater than the word *great* can tell, but because He is something more than "great." He is more than greatness, also more than love, power, or even goodness. That is, He is more than all of His attributes. No need to count the waves—simply jump in and swim.

Then you perceive that the ocean of Spirit pervades everything and is the very life of life. This essence by which the eye sees, the ear hears, the mouth speaks, the hand moves, the mind perceives, is Him. It is the Lord and the Lord alone.

Practice Exercise

As you relax and become still, preparing for a new experience of conscious oneness with Him, the all-pervading peace and bliss, feel the inner light and rhythm and harmony that flow through your body now as life and power. Let your body feel physically in tune with your own natural beingness.

Let your mind enjoy a sense of wonder at its own

limitless ability to think and to know. Let the harmony of the inner Christ-Mind fill your thoughts. Let your mind flow with divine love. Be at peace, be at peace.

As you remain in this state of tranquillity and balance, know for yourself:

My spiritual power is in repose. I flow peacefully with divine law. I rest in the ocean of divine love.

Imagine that you are floating easily, swimming effortlessly in a vast ocean of pure consciousness/bliss. There is nothing in the world to fear or resist. Be at peace now and experience this through imagination.

Meditate on this sense of being buoyed up by divine love and wisdom. The ocean of His presence enfolds and uplifts you now and forever. Like an open jar afloat on an endless sea of light and peace, the power and divine nature of the Lord flow freely throughout your being. You are in the ocean, and the ocean is in you—purifying you and giving you sweet peace and understanding from within. Rest in it, be cleansed and comforted. Rest in it, be lovingly carried with the current of spiritual unfoldment.

You can now travel through the experiences of life ever more fully aware of this current, this divine order and direction, which through all things and circumstances is leading you to your highest good. Words or phrases may come to you in your practice during the month that arise from the Christ-Mind in you, indicating to you the activity of divine law in your life. These insights should be recorded in your Spiritual Diary and kept in mind as you continue on this path. Give thanks that all the streams and rivers of life are ever flowing toward the ocean of infinite consciousness.

Learning Right Judgment
A NINTH STEP

As you take up this ninth step, give thanks for your growing ability to see the Truth and to make it your own in consciousness. As you think of the past lessons in this series, perhaps you can recognize that the material does indeed arrange itself in your experience not just as patterns of words and paragraphs on pages, but as patterns of insights and significant responses on your part that make this study alive, beautiful, and real. The ability to stand back from life and say: "Yes! I am making progress. I am becoming wiser, freer, happier . . . I am getting somewhere!"—to perceive these patterns of growth in your own life expression, is certainly a great gift of Spirit. This ability is the evidence of the blossoming of spiritual discrimination, that inner power of right discernment through which the mind divides the real from the unreal, the Truth from the illusion. Through this divine gift of clear vision you gain eternal freedom and peace.

Lesson 1: The Point

A person who has had to make some important decision in life may explain by saying, "I simply came to the point where something had to change, where I couldn't take it any longer, and where I finally saw the light." For whatever reason, because of whatever outer events, because of whatever the elements or persons involved in the situation, the individual who made the decision came to some conclusion, ventured on a choice. It may seem that outer things and other people were the reason that the individual had to make such a choice, but it must always be remembered that for each and every one, this is a world of mind. All is experienced, all is known, and all judgments and realizations come through the mind.

Events and circumstances and people may seem to have been responsible for this mind "coming to a point," but really it was something in the mind itself: a certain outlook or perspective, a judgment of the elements involved, a feeling or attitude that could not wait any longer to come forth, a kind of birth experience. (Who can tell how long the seed of a certain decision or judgment has been waiting in the fertile soil of a human mind?)

A certain sense of relief seems to come in everyone's experience after such a "point" has been reached, acknowledged, and passed successfully. There is a sense of growth, of emergence, of new beginning; there is a feeling that the activity of reaching some "point," and then making a positive choice of some kind, is a necessary part of all human development. Life *is* coming to these points. They are like mountain peaks in each one's personal ongoing. Greet the decisions and the overcomings in life with joy and assurance, for they mark the pathway to Self-realization.

When individuals say, "I came to the point . . . " they often mean that they came to a stop and then initiated some kind of change. It can mean more than just outer change; it can mean an inner realization of the true nature of things. When the choices that emerge from such a point in experience are based on Truth, then the changes that come about are positive and freeing. Otherwise, the individuals involved will become more and more entangled in the kind of mistaken identity that always brings suffering. Sooner or later, so long as a person refuses to come to such a stopping place, an evaluation point, he must travel around on the merry-go-round of self-determined cause and effect until he reaches the point.

There is no doubt that human life necessarily means continual decision-making: from which toy to play with, to which companion to choose, to which possession to buy, to what path to take to realize the spiritual potential. The most fundamental beginnings of education start with activities designed to develop the ability to discriminate accurately, to discern the differences between things. Society acknowledges that this is the beginning of learning; what it may not always recognize is the continual, evermore challenging and inspiring aspect of this quality of right discernment. It is a spiritual faculty with which all are endowed. It is the door-opening, cloud-chasing, dawn-hastening activity of mind whereby Reality is known and enjoyed.

This longing for wisdom and right understanding is present in each and all, waiting to be discovered and given room. Yet the unawakened mind is so preoccupied with sensual and material existence that it is dazzled, confused by the myriad choices that appearances present. It is often dulled or absorbed by the outer show of the world, not yet having listened to the inner urging to come up higher for a better look at things. The mind that is consciously unfolding, however, is not dulled, and perceives choices and alternatives where others may not; still more and more it rests in an inner knowing that the right way is being revealed. The mind that is consciously unfolding feels the urgency of spiritual progress where others may not yet feel this urgency, but it also begins to feel a peace about things. Regardless of anyone's behavior, though, the ability to judge rightly is slowly and surely opening within each being like a hidden, perfect rose.

In the realm of effects, it would seem that there are

more choices to be made by human beings in this modern world of advertising than we have ever had to face before. But the countless subtle choices of life have been present always. The increase in material objects for sale, or the great variety of other choices in the commercial world, only emphasize the need for the development of the faculty of judgment in people. More or fewer choices made available at the marketplace have nothing whatever to do with whether or not there is peace or stress in life.

Suffering comes when the faculty of right judgment is not well developed. Eliminating most of the choices of modern life would not really eliminate mental anguish. This suffering does not result from outer things, but from the natural inner demand for a higher criterion of choice than the senses or reasoning can provide. Many have been disappointed to find that simplifying outer existence—even down to the bare essentials—has not guaranteed inner tranquillity. (Robinson Crusoe faced all kinds of great decisions!) In a way, people have fabricated this great display of choice, demanding standards in order to exercise the ability that they inwardly sense is so vital to their growth. And each one must come to the awareness that so long as there is confusion about one's real identity, there may be confusion in making any kind of choice—whether the choices involve great corporations, investments, marriages, or career matters, or whether the choice be to eat a carrot or a potato for lunch. The subtle unrest will be there so long as the mind does not know the real Source of all its power or the real meaning of life.

This real meaning is the life of life, the reason and the Truth behind it all. Some beginners mistake the first part of metaphysics to be the whole: that the mind (thinking) results in all outer manifestations in the world, creating and changing effects according to consciousness. This is only the start of metaphysics. Seek deeper with all your mind and heart to the inner Light that lights it all. Reaching one stopping point, be restless to go on from there to the foundation of all worldly knowledge and all metaphysics as well.

Realize the Source of all finite mind—that changeless, radiant Beingness. Once that realization is attained, this outer world drops its veil for you. In every kind of choice, the self-realized soul beholds the loving Teacher of all. Only this eternal essence stands behind the world of appearances, waiting to be fully known. Whatever else you may do in life, above everything, choose the path of God-realization; as the heart opens to Him, the mind clears.

Through the suffering and frustration that result when individuals cannot seem to arrive at a positive decision about their life and affairs, that inner self of each one is silently and subtly pleading, "Please, come to the point!" This is surely what you would think if someone were trying to tell you something or perform some task, and he continually digressed from the subject or seemed to forget the purpose. You would eventually want to shout, "Get to the point!" And what is the point of it all? It is the *idea* of the thing—the goal. What is the idea behind or the goal of all creation? It is conscious unity with God. What is the idea behind or the true goal of your life?

It is conscious unity with God. When the urgency of some decision seems to press heavily upon you, give even a few seconds to the thought of this inner God-with-you urging you, "Get to the point of all life, beloved," and the decision will work out in a right and beautiful way.

That divine Self of you will never leave you. In deep sleep, the ego and its limited sense of identity is absent. The sleeper does not know if he is man or woman, married or unmarried, young or old, rich or poor, educated or uneducated. All sense of experience, past or present, has vanished. Still the Light of consciousness shines.

The alarm clock signals the awakening of the ego-sense and at once the individual feels: I am so-and-so; I live in this place; I have such-and-such a position and duties in life, friends, likes, and dislikes. Countless judgments about one's self and one's life spring to the surface of the active mind. Yet that Light of consciousness shines beneath and beyond all this as the absolute Truth, the standard for all right judgment. The outer things all change, by-and-by. The body changes, the mind changes, too, as the passage of events goes on. And all this time in timelessness the Light of consciousness shines. The finite mind is dependent on experience, on the influences of the world; the infinite Mind expressed through man is direct knowing, changeless and perfect, lighting all humanity.

What a prize is human life! Even with all its decisions and challenges, how wonderful it is! War and conflict, hunger and oppression, poverty and ignorance still occur in this world, but always, even in the darkest corner of human existence, there is the eternal possibility for a better life.

Resolve to live that better life for which you were born. Make up your mind and heart now, come to that point of your being that is all Light, all wisdom. In approaching the very idea of attaining the full power of right judgment, it is good to assume and seek to maintain the attitude of a witness—seeing things as they are and taking from each experience the best that is there. That which shines within you as all-wise, all-loving Being is the witness of all things. Draw the mind back into the witness seat and let this Light fill your awareness.

Practice Exercise

As you attempt to relax and prepare physically and mentally for this practice exercise, do not be concerned if you feel a little restless. Speak to your senses and your thinking and feeling nature in a soothing way, saying inwardly: "It is all right, do not struggle. The new strength and realizations you seek will come about now in an easy, pleasant way." It is not necessary to force the mind; let it go and it will come full circle back to the point again. Do not work hard to concentrate, just think for a moment of this spiritual Light shining within you now and always without work or struggle; and as you begin to think of this, understanding about everything will come to you naturally.

It is often difficult to willfully fix the mind on one point only. Even though you may be determined to experience the point of Light within your being, don't fight any resistance you feel; just let the mind play like a child, but keep watchful of your thoughts. Become like an architect's compass in the sense that no matter where the pencil point travels, the point of the compass remains fixed. Think of this illustration. Feel inwardly fixed and centered, yet free. Follow the wanderings of the mind for a few moments, but at the same time maintain the awareness of the inner point of Light.

Soon it becomes easier to keep the sense of being gently but firmly anchored in a timeless all-knowingness. Let the mind be free to form endless circle after circle of thought. But remember that at the very center of your consciousness shines that point of eternal Light. Know with peace and assurance:

The Christ light of wisdom and right judgment concerning all things shines forever within me, guiding my way.

Give thanks that whatever decisions present themselves to you, however many choices you need to make in your life and affairs, you can make them all wisely and peacefully because of your spiritual stability. Trust in this center of all wisdom within you. When you think, speak, and act from this center, the harmonizing, uplifting, and miracle-manifesting power of God is mighty with you and through you.

If certain decisions should trouble you, remember

this Light within. (No matter if you think others might think some of these things are trivial—this is just for you.) Be sure to write these decisions or questions down in your Spiritual Diary, addressing everything to the all-knowing Self of you. Pause to look at the words you have written. Then close your eyes and begin to draw the "pencil point" of your thinking and feeling back to this center, this inner compass point that has never moved. After a moment, write this after the question or problem and trustingly affirm it:

The Christ light in me reveals all things in right relationship. The Christ of my being protects and directs me. The Christ reveals the right way.

Give thanks instantly, for the right answer clears in your awareness and you are unfolding in wisdom and power as you remain centered in this radiant point of Christ light.

Learning Right Judgment
A TENTH STEP

Because of your unfolding sensitivity to spiritual things and to individuals everywhere, all consciously or unconsciously seeking this same Ideal, you perceive that life holds the old eternal choices, possibilities, and infinite potential for all. You see more completely than ever before, that the most basic needs of life, the underlying longings and questionings, are essentially the same for souls in every age, in every place. There is a universally shared experience—a shared restlessness from within. The restlessness grows into a wondering, and the wondering into an active seeking, and the active seeking into love—devotion to the Truth. This love unfolds from within outward as the Answer that answers everything.

Lesson 2: Love, the Divine Answer

The miracle of it all is that the divine Answer is forever seeking to reveal itself to everyone everywhere. It is seeking to reveal itself to you now, in all that you experience, through everyone that you meet, through these words now, and through all the words that you study and listen to as you glean for Truth.

If you find sweetness in reading scriptures or other Truth writings, if you find yourself pausing just after some phrase to lift up your eyes from the page or close them in a brief moment of peace and wonder that comes to you suddenly through the medium of the words (you can't tell just how), be grateful for this experience of divine grace. This is the love of Truth actively growing and unfolding in you. This love is itself the great affirmation of all that you have ever heard that is good and true and eternal. And it is the continual denial of all that may seem depressing or limiting to you in any way, either in thoughts of the past, the present, or the future. This unfolding love is the living process of affirmation and denial active in your life. It is ever choosing through you and for you experiences and relationships and directions in life that are filled with possibilities of greatness.

Grace—divine love in action—is signaled by your seeking, and it comes to fruition as a peaceful self-reliance in all that you undertake. Learn to think lovingly of the universe; actively seek the spiritual Ideal—the divine Beloved—in all that you do, and you will be safe, illumined, free.

As any serious decision confronts you, try to feel this inner freedom and self-reliance; sense the peaceful inner knowing that is love expressed. Try to develop a sense of devotion and oneness with Spirit even before you actually formulate a specific choice in the matter at hand. Seek to feel devotion for the spiritual Ideal—for God, for the Christ of your being, for that radiant Self, for the universal Father or Mother or Friend, for whatever form or attributes this Beingness assumes for you. The love you experience for that which is the highest and best will begin to illumine all your sensibilities with wisdom and confidence. Love will transmute your attitudes for the better; it will change and uplift you. Love will light your life.

As you seek out the answers to life's questions, and as you develop an attitude of love even through the hardest lessons, you see more and more that all these things must be discovered by each one for himself. No one can learn for another. There is no standard book of etiquette that will be an infallible guide through all the shadows and turns of your life. Therefore, strive to get at the very base of all the lessons—that self-luminous Self of you.

Remember always that no matter who may hold up diplomas before you, whoever may tell of great visions, whoever has made miraculous overcomings and turns back to tell you about them, whoever expounds beautiful scriptures and great teachings, the final answer to your questions must always come from the timeless Self of *you* and none other. No one else has timeless answers for those old questions.

The illumined souls of all time have always taught this Truth. They have always pointed to the I AM of your very own being as the source of all wisdom. This Christ Spirit is the Way and the Truth and the Light forever. Follow this Light.

Sooner or later, you will begin to experience a genuine devotion blossoming from within whenever you think about the spiritual Ideal, whenever you think about Truth. Think about this feeling of love and inspiration. This is the Answer trying to come through, and it is trying to come through even in the hardest decisions as wisdom and peace.

It becomes natural and progressively easy to love and become consciously at one with that which is the Answer to all questions, the remedy revealed, the treasure continually offered, the Beloved that your mind and heart have been seeking to know all along. Only that which is love itself can permanently attract and fulfill the deepest desire of your heart, the boundless love you have to express. Seek this ultimate Answer through all the judgments and decisions of your life.

Reflect for a moment about what it is like to be in love. No, this kind of reverie is not really out of place in learning right judgment. (After all, the wise, the clear-eyed are always in love with life.) And it is not out of place in religion—not in true religion. Those who have been recognized as saints and seers of every faith have been God-intoxicated, cosmically "in-love" individuals. They have known love so fully that the experience has transformed their life and the lives of countless others. Think of this ecstasy!

The one who knows this love—who is in love with the spiritual Ideal—will always choose to think about, to be consciously with, to see remembrances of the Beloved in each and every thing and circumstance. The matter of deciding whether or not to dwell upon the Beloved is simply not considered. The mind and heart of the devotee follow naturally and gladly toward the Beloved at all times.

The practice of positive affirmation and denial is an important way to help the spiritual aspirant direct and uplift the mind so that more and more it will naturally and gladly dwell on the spiritual Ideal. It is important to remember that the right use of affirmation and denial is not for the ultimate purpose of strengthening the mental powers nor of producing certain desired effects in the realm of appearances. What a dangerous pitfall this false concept can be! Rather, the right use of affirmation and denial is to develop the faculty of spiritual discrimination—the clear sense of what is unreal and what is Real. The development of right judgment, spiritual discrimination, leads to the blooming of devotion. Complete liberation—unity with the spiritual Ideal in thought, word, and action—is the fruit of devotion.

With the idea in mind of developing the love faculty of your being, and with the confidence that the development of this faculty will naturally and beautifully develop also the judgment faculty, let the beloved Spirit, the Christ of your being, lead you always. As you enter into the creative process of affirmation and denial, know that it is the Beloved you seek to experience, the Beloved you seek to express. Know that the beloved Christ of your being intends only blessings and ever greater realization for you through all that you encounter in life. The answer trying to come through for you now is real and important and meaningful for you in the life situations you experience in day-to-day unfoldment. Therefore, free yourself to formulate and use affirmations and denials that mean something to you at your own particular point in unfoldment, as you pass through this particular growth process. Lovingly and firmly devise your own statements yourself, inspired by the Teacher within. Or, still led by this same Teacher, choose statements that you have read or heard which really *speak* those inner feelings you have. Your Teacher is ever seeking to guide and instruct you through everything and everyone.

Be persistent as you strive for inner peace and sureness. Write, repeat, think your statements to yourself until you can get the same sense of sureness and peace that accompanies real love—mother or father for child, child for parent, friend for friend, lover for beloved.

Get at the essence of pure love in your mind and heart. Then do not lose touch with the value of this experience; bring it out into the light of today. Find it when you need it most: in trouble, in indecision, in doubt, in confusion, in fear, in all life.

This Truth that you love is not out of place in life.

Sometimes you may feel out of place with the lessons. But when you can get at the meaning of life's lessons, and when you can feel love welling up in your thoughts and feelings and judgments about things—even if the pieces don't seem to fit together in the outer yet—just trust in this feeling. Let it guide your words and actions. And let the outcome take care of itself. It will!

Practice Exercise

As you begin this practice exercise, put the pressing decisions of life aside for the moment, and as you relax and become attuned to the guidance of your inner Self, feel that in all things the supreme Beloved of your soul is comforting, uplifting, and directing you.

Breathe in the love that the Self eternally gives to you, and as you breathe out easily and freely, know that the divine love you are experiencing is naturally expressing into every area of your life. Even in unseen ways, the answers you seek are being made manifest.

Now that you are relaxing and feeling receptive, let your mind flow to the feeling of deep love. If you have ever felt "in love," give thanks for the blessing that is the essence of this feeling. Let the remembrance of love be lifted in your thinking, completely out of the context of sentimentality or emotionalism. Realize that the faculty of pure love with which you are spiritually endowed is really one with the faculty of perfect judgment. Both are of the Christ nature.

Take the feeling of love into the silence of your being and see what answers it has for you. Lift it up into the heights of your highest thoughts. Direct it toward the Beloved that is the light of every person and every experience. Let that pure love illumine your judgment faculty. Feel how, like a great warm and loving light, it seeks to reveal everything to you.

How wonderful to have every decision life brings your way answered with such a feeling! If only you could lift up your eyes from every problem and test of life with such a sureness and peace, and if only you could proceed in every judgment and choice prompted by divine love. Beloved child of God, this is your birthright and destiny.

In order to begin to claim this birthright, use the creative method of affirmation and denial with the spirit of devotion so that your judgment faculty may be illumined. Use affirmation as a way of saying: *Yes! This is of the nature of my Beloved. I accept this with all my mind and heart!* Use denial as a way of saying: *No! This is not of the nature of my Beloved. I bar this from my consciousness!* In this way the spiritual aspirant becomes truly free and divinely wise. In this way you will come to know the Beloved of your soul as never before.

For example, if you seek illumination concerning a health challenge, try this technique of seeking the Christ essence even in the midst of the illness experience. You might use an affirmative statement, such as:

My true nature is one with the nature of Spirit, the Beloved of my mind and heart. Therefore, I, too, am essentially whole, strong, eternal, beautiful, and vitally alive. I accept this Truth with all my mind and heart.

And you might accompany this statement with a denial, such as:

The appearance of illness or weakness that I have been experiencing is in no way a part of the nature of Spirit, the Beloved of my mind and heart. Therefore, I do not accept or give power in word, thought, or action to the appearance of illness. I declare this appearance as a challenge to be overcome victoriously, a passing growth experience.

The outcome of both the affirmation and the denial should be an increased tendency to dwell on the qualities of Spirit. This tendency of mind and heart will be experienced and outpictured as the perfection of Spirit.

If a problem concerning personal relationships with other people has developed in your life, purify your judgment faculty with the same technique. Try a statement like this:

My true nature and the true nature of each individual concerned in this situation are one with the true nature of Spirit, the Beloved of the universe. Therefore, we are essentially loving, wise, understanding, harmonious, and patient. I accept this Truth with all my mind and heart.

And try also a freeing statement of denial, such as:

The apparent antagonism, conflict, or lack of communication in this situation in no way reveals the true nature of all concerned, which is the peace and love and wisdom of Spirit, the Beloved of the universe. I do not accept or give power in my thought, word, or deed to these negative conditions, and I declare this problem as a passing growth experience, a challenge to be overcome with victory and love.

The outcome of both the affirmation and the denial should once again be a new revelation and attraction to the qualities of Spirit. By dwelling on these spiritual qualities, the mind becomes infused with light. Drawn by love, the mind is uplifted into a new, ever more perfect wisdom and peace. The companions you attract and the experiences you share with others will express the love in your mind and heart.

If you are seeking right judgment concerning prosperity in your affairs, perhaps this kind of statement will prove very helpful:

My true nature is the nature of Spirit, the Beloved of my mind and heart. I am rich in ideas and creative ability and I express and attract abundance. I accept this Truth with all my mind and heart.

And this type of denial may also help:

This appearance of lack is in no way my natural state, for it is not of the nature of Spirit, the Beloved of my mind and heart, the Source of infinite supply. Therefore, I do not accept or give power in my thought, word, or action to this negative appearance, and I declare this appearance as a passing growth experience, a challenge through which the Beloved will be demonstrated in full glory.

As before, the outcome of the affirmation and the denial noted should be that more and more thought and feeling are centered on the positive qualities of the Beloved, the Christ nature. Naturally, as thoughts are outpictured by the universal law of mind action, those positive qualities will come to the surface of your experience. Perhaps the answers and the outworking will come in ways that surprise you—even in ways that challenge you further. Only good can come of this seeking activity. Therefore, trust in the leading of Spirit. When you are challenged by indecision or contradictory appearances, love more. Think of the spiritual qualities of the Beloved of your mind and heart for even a few solid seconds a day, and your life will fill with new light. Beloved, bless your Spiritual Diary as you write your personal affirmations and denials there. It will reveal wonderful things to you about yourself and about the Christ self of you. Bless you as the divine answer comes through for you ever more clearly and freely. Now and forever, you are unfolding!

*Facets of
Self-Unfoldment*

AN
ELEVENTH STEP

As a consciously unfolding soul, you may perceive that not only the young and the seemingly inexperienced may cry for higher guidance in this world; those who have lived longer in this life expression and have given a try to many more angles in life may also cry out just as urgently for higher guidance. Everyone seems to be straining at the same old questions: What is useful/useless? What is good/bad? What is right/wrong?

How like the balance-point of a scale is that slash mark between useful and useless, good and bad, right and wrong! The idealist might like to see only one side of the scale and deal only with the useful, the good, and the right. These positive aspects are the nature of Reality in the absolute sense. Every Truth student is an idealist at heart. How beautiful to behold in all the world only the purity and light! This purity and light, this usefulness, goodness, and rightness are *there,* to be sure—for the eyes that are unveiled, for the clear-seeing. But also vital are those rare and courageous individuals who are willing to wrestle with appearances wherever a real contest is called for in this world now, in this place, yet still keep their idealism, their inner vision of light. Will you be one of those rare individuals?

Lesson 1: The Balance-Point

As the idealist enters the path of conscious self-unfoldment, he needs to become aware of the other side of the scale, too. He must recognize appearances for what they are so that he can see the shining ideal more perfectly as the spiritual potential for all life. Without this kind of balance in judgment, the idealist becomes a mere stereotype: a dreamer in a private ivory tower, head in the clouds, unmindful that his tower may be on very shaky ground indeed. Here is where the practical side of the mind must come in. The one who takes the active approach to life as it is lived and experienced here and now sees where appearances do not yet outpicture the Ideal, and he steps in lovingly and fearlessly to do the work of reforming and uplifting. Can you make this kind of decision and follow it through in your own life situations?

This is the kind of decision that is the groundwork and the balance-point for the operation of the choosing faculty of your mind in all the other areas of your life. The first prerequisite is that you must be willing to put the past—starting from the minute that has just slipped by—altogether behind you and begin with the *now*. Life may have seemed dark for you, but there is a new day dawning now. It may even have seemed that you had to contend with a great many rascals and fools (perhaps you have even played these parts yourself at one time or another). Never mind; you shall be one of the clear-eyed. You shall be free.

What is it, after all, that makes a person a rascal or a fool? Surely it is only a narrow view of things, an unbalanced approach of selfishness, fear, resentment, insecurity. All these attitudes arise ultimately out of a wrong concept of what one's true identity and divine nature are. Have you ever known or been such an unhappy person? Then you will know from the depths of the humanness that all people share with you that even at the base of apparent meanness lies a feeling of being lost and out of touch, an unsureness about what one really wants out of life, and an ignorance of what truly remarkable things one can do and expect out of life. These challenging feelings are for the purpose of learning and growth. Even a miserable feeling is a blessing, a great lesson trying to come through.

Consciously or unconsciously, in creative ways or

in seemingly destructive ways, everyone everywhere is seeking the Truth, the genuine—Reality. No one, nothing in the world escapes unfoldment. A little child will spin around and around in play, enjoying the dizziness. But sooner or later the child will tumble to the ground, or he will get enough of it and stop himself and sit a minute. After a short time, the dizziness subsides and the normal sense of balance is naturally restored. This is what is necessary to anyone who consciously takes up this spiritual life—finally to get enough of the aimless spinning and to learn a little stillness, find a little peacefulness, and practice a little equanimity. The head will begin to clear, the heart will calm, and the innate spiritual balance will begin to be restored. Then the "child" can get up and go about his play with new energy and purpose.

But, to be sure, the spinning around is fun and interesting—up to a point. Do not feel too remorseful if after having attained a certain amount of spiritual poise you find yourself spinning around in the realm of appearances again, feeling suddenly lost and confused. Spiritual development is cyclic; be patient with yourself and with others. Do not judge too harshly. A patient attitude is necessary to right judgment in everything. The important thing to remember is that once having touched on this inner realm, once having learned something of the art of silence and creative thinking and feeling, you can always regain this sense of balance. Only desire it and be willing to give even a little of yourself in this direction and the rewards will come. Things of Spirit can never be lost, only temporarily forgotten. Do as the child does: sit down a minute.

Feeling lost, return again to thoughts of the spiritual Ideal. Sit down and become still physically, if possible, and by all means, emotionally and mentally. Let your idealism give force to your living, and let that inner Self of you give balance. The sureness about every facet of life will emerge not as a hazy possibility, but as a real and workable way of life.

Remember that religion, or Truth, or whatever name you would like to give to this seeking that starts inward and spins out into eternity, must be practical, livable, real as a heartbeat.

When you are faced with a "heartbeat" decision in life, perhaps the first thing that you might be told is, "Be reasonable about this . . . use your reason . . . reason it out." Philosophers may state that any kind of metaphysics or transcendentalism is out of place in pure reasoning. And yet, in order to "reason," even the strictest philosophers will agree that one must "step back" from the elements of the problem at hand.

They indicate that a kind of mental balance is necessary, and they might use somewhat different terms to describe the needed transcendence from the emotional biases or inaccurate perceptions that may cloud the valid answer. This "clear air" is sought by the common man and the intellectualist, the religionist and the so-called practical individual. Perhaps what must first be transcended is the old semantic tie-up! The goal seems really to be the same for all.

As you seek to "reason things out," try to seek a

balance in your own mind. Be self-reliant. Manage to step back—better, step *up*. Transcend the old concepts of what you may have been told is the most reasonable approach to a problem, or to life as a whole. Dare to be cold and calculating when it feels right to you. At the same time, dare also to be warm and accepting and positive, even beyond what the "facts" may seem to call for, when that feels right to you.

Get free of the notion that you are the kind of person who must always follow your head or follow your heart. Let *all* of your divine faculties be fully alive. Be versatile, changing as life is. You can dare to be changing and open, for you are inwardly grounded in the changeless Reality that lies at the heart of it all. You do not need to limit yourself to the belief that you are exclusively either a thinking or a feeling person. Approach decision with receptivity, with readiness to find beauty and Truth in all the facets of your life experience. Discover the answers for yourself. Trust yourself; think for yourself.

You can operate from the balance-point between so-called opposite ways of problem-solving. What is the balance-point between "cold reason" and "blind optimism"? What is the equalizer, the translator? It is the "given" in all of existence. Words cannot pin down this "given," but perhaps the old standard statement of Truth is the best way to try:

There is but one Presence and one Power in the universe, God, the good omnipotent.

This is really the base from which all right reasoning ought to begin, for it is the root of all knowledge, the essence of Truth.

If you can accept this "given" as the balance-point of your own consciousness, you will be out of danger of tipping over into the sea of outer appearances, confusing sense impressions, contradictory "facts," and you will be equally safe from the danger of slipping off balance in the other way—to flounder in emotionalism, groundless wishful thinking, baseless fears and doubts. You will become ever more sure and clear-eyed. You will become free.

Practice Exercise

Become relaxed, at ease. Let the physical body assume the equilibrium of a scale perfectly in balance. Let the spine be straight, and the shoulders even; relax especially the neck and face. Try placing the hands just above the knees or upon the arms of your chair. Let the hands relax, palms open upward, fingers and wrists as calm and peaceful as possible. Perhaps you might like to put these pages aside for a few moments at this time and assume this attitude of physical balance in order to feel the meanings it has for you. Take your time.

It is hoped that this physical attitude will begin to make you feel emotionally and mentally balanced and ready. It is as if the entire body is now making the statement. *I am at peace, I am at peace. I am stabilized. I am ready now to experience the fullness of the Truth of my being.*

You may want to make a special note of this experience in your Spiritual Diary. In times of great emotional distress and mental confusion—grief, indecision, turmoil—practice of this physical position, with mindfulness of the inner states of equanimity that it is intended to suggest and reveal, will bring helpful results.

By this point in time, when you sit down to work with the practice exercise, your mind will most often enter into a peaceful, receptive state almost automatically. Without losing that peaceful receptivity to inner revelation, try also to keep aware of the decision-making process that is continuing, continuing—so much a part of your everyday life. Without fear of being distracted from your high spiritual purpose in this practice, let the perimeters of your consciousness observe the most pressing decisions of your life now: emotional, mental, financial, family, *life* problems.

Is there something you do not feel quite happy about in your life? Face it squarely now in your thinking and feeling. Just by doing this balanced, honest, peaceful, "facing" activity, you may find that many so-called problems clear almost immediately and begin instantly to work themselves out in your life and affairs. Perhaps much of the uneasiness you have been experiencing concerning some particular area of your life has really resulted from your not facing it completely. Ask yourself, "How do I feel about this . . . what is the problem?"

First step: decline to be a problem or a problem-maker yourself. Resolve to work with the right and peaceful outworking of any problem situation. Let a feeling of love emerge through this experience. Having sat down with the problem, become still and let the dizziness about it subside. Allow the inner spiritual balance to be restored naturally and easily, beginning right now.

If there are no particular urgent choices before you at present, think of the discriminative faculty of your being, of how necessary and important its development is to your spiritual unfoldment. Think of the divine gift of the ability to choose with sureness and peace. Bless all your faculties of thinking and feeling. Give thanks that your mind's eye is clearing now to perfect vision.

As these thoughts pass through the mind, be sure to remain watchful over your physical body, too. Do not let tensions disturb your outer poise and balance. Keep the back straight and the whole frame controlled and peaceful. Let your body be an instrument for the experience and expression of Spirit.

In your mind's eye imagine that the words and meaning of the following affirmation are shining like a balance-bar along a line connecting your shoulders:

There is one Presence and one Power in the universe, God, the good omnipotent.

Perhaps there are two main possible approaches to some decision that is before you, or perhaps there are two prominent personalities coming into play in the situation in your mind. Whatever the elements of any decision may be, bring them into the realm of your immediate experience. Deal with them not through reason alone, and not just emotionally, but let the spiritual faculty of your being take the lead. Let all these thoughts come into full focus in your mind without any of the tension that may have restricted a peaceful and right answer before.

Think of the tools of affirmation and denial: both are great lights toward spiritual realization. Mentally place affirmation upon one of your hands, denial upon the other. Remember, you are not weighing one specific approach to a certain problem against the other, nor one person against the other. Instead, the purpose is to clear the mind concerning all these elements. On the one hand, do not deny persons or particular methods to solving the problem, but deny firmly and peacefully the fearful thoughts or the negative reactions that you may have been holding. On the affirmation side, do not attempt to choose at this instant either a person or a specific action. Affirm the attributes of the beloved Christ essence; know that the Christ is the loving activity through everyone and through every element of the circumstance.

By affirming this essential Christ nature, you free it into activity in your own consciousness. This higher thinking is the seed of enlightened words and actions on your part. This uplifted approach is the peacemaker and the Way-Shower to all concerned. The answer will begin to come forth now, without pressure to anyone or anything, and even without anyone else knowing that you are working toward a solution in this way.

There is one Presence and one Power in the universe, God, the good omnipotent. Start with this, then you may reason out any problem deductively or inductively, and the answer will prove valid. With the exacting mind of the mathematician, eliminate the wrong answers without guilt feelings, peacefully and optimistically crossing out the mistakes along the way, eager to proceed toward the right conclusion. Keep at it until you have it right. Always keep pure love alive: love for the right answer, for it is beautiful, eternal, true, right there for the knowing and the expressing.

How circular the whole thing turns out to be! For the "given" at the beginning is revealed to be the ultimate answer and outcome of it all. The answer has been there all along. The inner balance really has never been disturbed. Become in accord with this equanimity, and your vision will clear, your life purpose and direction will unfold.

God is blessing you now from within your very being; you are divinely endowed with peace, poise, and balance. You are a beloved, clear-eyed child of the loving Mother-Father God, and you are forever unfolding!

Facets of Self-Unfoldment
A TWELFTH STEP

Your arrival at your present wonderful awareness of Truth is most assuredly the work of the Holy Spirit— of grace, God's love in action. This eternal, wisdom-revealing force and Presence has been at work through every teaching you have grown through and in every teacher who has touched your life with divine fire.

What have all the great teachers, all the saints lived for and made known their ecstacy for, if not for you and others like you? For what purpose has the spiritual path been lighted by them, if not that *you* should walk there yourself?

Even as you read, divine energies rush to aid your unfoldment, angelic forces enfold you with protecting presence, and the Lord of your being—personal and real—is keeping a loving eye on you, is pleased with you, and longs to reveal all Truth to you.

Last Lesson: Your Teacher

The distinction between consciously seeking persons and others in the world is that awakened souls are not content to wait, inactive, while the inexorable law of the universe establishes order in their sphere, but rather they choose to understand this law and become attuned to it. The motive of the true seeker is not merely to avoid the suffering that comes with ignorance of divine principle, not only to become adept in the naturally success-attracting applications of Truth, but simply to become consciously attuned to divine law, Truth—to God, all joy and all peace—and all for love.

It is the nature of the true seeker to ultimately find and follow the highest teaching for the sincere love of Truth, and to become the intimate disciple of the one true Teacher. Therefore, become like a child in your willingness and readiness to find this Teacher, to follow the path of spiritual life as it unfolds through grace according to your own unique nature.

As you extend your hand in spirit, ready to walk in consciousness with many outer teachers, many spiritual companions on the path, keep your childlike sensibilities. Think how guileless is a child's nature.

Think how no one knows so well as pure children when they are really loved. No one can detect a false-hood more quickly than a child. No one is more eager to share in genuine love, the excitement of discovery, the pleasantness of peace and openness, and the wonder of growing. You are that ideal child in Truth, and you shall be safe and sure of happy outcomes as you express this spontaneous unfolding spirit.

Because you are a renewed child in Spirit, miracles are the natural and expected course of events for you. So if you expect miracles along the spiritual path, you shall certainly have them. But mind that, if you insist on obvious, even spectacular miracles in life, you do not overlook miracles half-hidden in the everyday, but real just the same. Have you counted the miracles of every natural breath you have so casually been taking while reading this page; or the miracle that each precious molecule of oxygen you inhale so nonchalantly from the air is carried by un-seen obedient travelers in the bloodstream (a great miracle itself!) to nourish untold numbers of tiny perfect cells in your wondrous body, all in a divinely ordered pattern of life; or the miracle that there are others—countless others—in every kind of place on this globe (perhaps other globes as well) who are seeking the same bright goals you are now seeking, and finding them? If you are not awestricken and thrilled through and through at such miracles, how can lesser events in the world of appearances possibly move you?

"Awake, O sleeper," the Teacher within com-mands. Start with developing a greater sensitivity to the profound miracles that are as close to you now as breath or the layers of sensitive skin that envelop the life stuff of your body temple. Then see what other great signs are soon revealed to you. When you feel insistent on a "sign" from Spirit, a message from the perfect Teacher, think a moment about the signs and messages you are given every instant of the night and day; signs ceaselessly flashing to you every microsecond of your existence that speak more eloquently than any words the eternal living message: *I love you. I breathe through you perfect life. I empower you for all greatness and grace you with all that is good, beloved one. I AM the very life of your life.*

This message is your innate and natural daily lesson material. Therefore, be natural about the business of spiritual unfoldment. Even as you breathe, as you eat and sleep, you are unfolding in a sure and certain process. Be serious about spiritual goals, but do not try too hard—don't strain at it. The steps in unfoldment will present themselves to you at the right time; they cannot be rushed or forestalled, and when they come, you will take them.

Think of the perfect child awaiting the moment of birth—peacefully growing, ceaselessly building in strength and readiness for that inevitable right time. Let there be no anxiety, no uncertainty about the natural process of unfoldment. Be at peace, for God is enfolding you with love, supplying you with spiritual nourishment, and preparing you for every great moment of spiritual birth.

As to the right path, the right teachers, the right method of spiritual research, you will find you develop a kind of craving for what you need when you need it. Follow your inner urgings. Then follow through by mustering the courage to take up any given technique or school of thought and carry it through to its ideal culmination; to become its champion, its exemplar, its perfect disciple, its spokesman and leader if need be. Become just as courageous also to set it aside and forget it peacefully as you travel onward, when it has served its purpose in your unfoldment.

The old warning still stands, the old reminder must be noted. Be free—follow only your Self. You are the servant of all, yet you have but one Master. You are the student of all, yet you have but one Teacher. Remain free in your heart of hearts, no matter how wholly on the outer you may give yourself to any teaching or teacher. Remain unattached inwardly from all save the Master of all masters, the Lord indwelling.

Against what standard shall you hold all the teachings, all the wise sayings, all the doctrines and prophecies, all the leaders and teachers that life presents to you? Against that alone which is changeless, against that alone which is ultimately reliable—this eternal self-existent, pure Self.

Against this ultimate standard you have a divinely inherent right to test everything and anything before you give your acceptance. Test not with small-mindedness and not by appearances. Otherwise, you may miss the wonderful teaching meant for you and pass over the great teacher who may hold golden keys to your own growth, simply on the basis of some insignificant judgment. What does it matter to you if a certain Truth teacher does not follow the diet you think is necessary, or if he or she does not always look or speak or act according to your present expectancies of a spiritual master? If spirituality is signaled in you in this teacher's presence, then follow *this* signal. The rest is unimportant and overemphasis on these minor appearances will attach you to the very things you wish to eliminate from your life and consciousness. Be free of this limitation, for you are meant for free unfoldment. Remember, it is not the body or the personality of your teachers in life that you are meant to be attached to; for Truth alone is your beloved, and you cannot remain fixed to anything or anyone else. Great teachers, like life itself (the greatest teacher), have a way of acting in unexpected ways, and they are not always predictable. Truth is many-faceted, and all facets must be known. Let the Truth be revealed in whatever ways it may, and rejoice in each new experience.

Rejoice in the fact that there are so many paths, so many teachers that each of us may choose the way to Truth that most suits our nature. Rejoice in the surface differences among all the methods set forth, and keep a sense of happiness about the outcomes for you as you follow the methods that feel right for you in this life.

Choose the methods to spirituality that most suit you in every phase of your life. As concerns your personal living habits, be careful but not harsh. Be as strict with yourself in these matters as seems right and necessary to you. Respect life, but do not be immobilized by fear of death or taint. Spirit, your true Source of life, is deathless and forever pure.

Respect your life well enough to be careful about preserving and protecting your natural vitality. Do not misuse your beautiful body temple. But do not make of it a prison either. Don't be restricted by an undue fear of less than perfect food or less than ideal living conditions. The Source of perfect nourishment resides innately in every atom of this universe, and the Ideal resides innately in every moment and place. Be nourished by this pure Source through all that you eat and breathe.

What do you suppose is the origin of your will to live? It is the eternally perfect and living Christ within you. Follow this spiritual Instructor concerning these things. Use spiritual discrimination about what you eat and drink, and about where you go and with whom you associate, and about how you live. But do not be anxious—this is not the nature of the beloved, your eternally free Self. Never attempt to enforce your own sensibilities about diet, life-style, or spiritual matters on another. You cannot be free unless you let yourself and all others be free. As individuals unfold naturally, all become confident enough in the Christ self in themselves and within others to be at peace about each one. Know that we have a perfect Master to lead and instruct us.

We should not expect another to be a perfect example of health, beauty, perfection for us. The inner Master is the one perfect example. Each must learn not to judge by appearances. The so-called sinner may be much more spiritual and pure than the so-called upright citizen. The invalid may be much closer in consciousness to perfect wholeness than the seemingly fit person. The miserable soul in the gutter may know a good deal more than the passersby about the meaning of life. All so-called "levels" of spiritual development can be transcended at one split-second touch of divine grace. All are free and pure already in Spirit, and the goal is to know and live this Truth.

Once you emerge as a Truth student, everyone and everything become your Teacher, for the divine Teacher is immanent in each and all, calling to you and leading you to full realization. The more "cosmic" your consciousness becomes, the more alert you become to the fact that the Teacher is present everywhere—more than present in an abstract sense, but also touchable and reaching now to touch you!

Often individuals search for a perfect master, an ultimate teaching. This is to be found only with your Self; but because of the outward search for Truth; but teaching, because of the persistent delving into books, the listening attitude of the ideal student, because of this manifest longing, the gift of grace is increasingly bestowed. This priceless gift is the indescribably growing perception of teachers and Truth teachings apparent in every place and in everyone—from the uncommon to the common. The incarnations of God as Teacher are truly more myriad than the new leaves of forests or the dense and cleansing raindrops of a heavy spring rain. The gift of grace is the awareness that the all-knowing Teacher of all teachers is with you always.

The secret remains the same—in order to recognize the great teaching or the great Teacher, become a great student. In order to receive divine directives, be open to and expectant of the divine. Be ever prepared to receive and to act upon the divine beckoning to you everywhere. Listen for the Master, watch for Him, and He will come to you.

Through this attitude, you shall be one of the great ones. You shall be one of the masters, one of the founders. When all the vital steps in Self-knowledge come along in your life, praise God, for you shall be able to take them. You were born at a certain time and in a certain place among certain individuals for wonderful reasons—for greater and more beautiful reasons than have yet been revealed.

Be grateful for your life—even with all its ups and downs. As much as possible, keep the spiritual goal in the forefront of your consciousness. It is a hard thing, to be sure, to ask you to try to forget entirely your pressing problems in life. All these outer things have their weight and meaning—perhaps more meaning in spiritual terms than you might have thought. But be certain of this, you *will* develop a divine forgetfulness of the tension, the intense pain, the tight bind of it all. These indescribable moments will come to you—gifts of grace. They come not like doses of some sweet potion to soothe you away from the reality of life, but rather they come like draughts of thirst-quenching elixir. Following such moments, the "burden" grows light, the solution comes more clearly, and the good is closer at hand. Taking these steps in Self-knowledge is assuming true mastery; it is "coming into your own" at last.

Think of sitting in a one-passenger sailboat out at sea, waiting for any trace of wind from any direction at all to move you. Just when the heat, the powerful undercurrent, or the stagnant surface of the sea might seem to hold you powerless, a sudden waft of pure air fills the sails. Tilt the rudder and lift the sail to catch the wind of Spirit fully, and you are off and free. This wind is grace, and it blows always.

As you sail on in the spiritual life, keep an eye for the real prizes in store. Always let the wind of Spirit lift you beyond the obvious, into the freedom of Truth. For example, overcoming depression is a vital step in Self-knowledge, while "aura-vision" is inconsequential. What good will it do a man if he can walk on water if he cannot correct his own bad habits? Many clairvoyants have serious problems in the areas of health, prosperity, and human relations. But those we call the "ever free"—the God-realized ones—may or may not have "psychic powers," yet they have sailed beyond these limitations, carried on by the activity of grace. You, too, are meant for wider seas.

Seek not psychic experience, but spiritual experience, mystical communion with the Self. While it is good to arrange your life to be more conducive to mystical experience, remember that the great mystics of the earth have often achieved union with the Absolute at the most unlikely times, in the midst of the most (apparently) antagonistic events. This is the nature of what is called mystical experience. It sweeps away the obstacles in a flash. It uses outwardly adverse conditions to its own advantage. Its law is not brought into effect by a certain set of stimuli always; rather, its law sets up the stimuli—Spirit gives all the signals. Its law is grace—divine love in action. When the longing is developed in you, spiritual revelations will make their own time and place in your life.

The key—the longing for Self-knowledge—develops with practice of Truth ideas; and you have longing for Truth, else why would you have read so far into these thoughts? There is awakening within you now the equal or surpasser to every great Truth teacher or writer or sage or saint or master. Therefore with peace and confidence unfurl the sails of your heart to receive the full, freeing force of Spirit.

Practice Exercise

Let the body feel relaxed and quiet as you sit straight, yet easily in your study place. Let the mind be tranquil, removed from all anxious concerns. As you begin, anticipate healing; anticipate new insight; anticipate freedom and peace. You are here to receive a very personal blessing from your own inner perfect Master.

As you prepare to meet the Master in consciousness, let the mind become calmer and calmer, and as you breathe with peaceful rhythm, let a warm, happy feeling flow through all areas of your being.

Think of this perfect Master seated at the center of your heart. Think of this radiant Presence, this light, this inexpressible joy. Without making any prayer at all, not even for healing or the answer to some problem in life, only think of this Presence; focus on this alone for as long a moment as you can.

It seems strange to go on from here, for what you have been practicing just now is really the secret of right meditation and answered prayer. Without attaching any limitation to the pure thought of this Presence, you lift your own consciousness into the spiritual vibration of the Christ. Here, all is answered, all is complete. If you can hold the mind to the Christ-focus, even for a second, you will see for yourself the great blessings that come through.

Through this activity, devotion is kindled in your mind and heart. Devotion to the spiritual Ideal is its own reward. It takes away the pain and confusion of challenging life experiences. The Christ of your being is truly the Great Physician. Lift your mind to be touched by this hand of light, and the healing you receive will be sure and complete.

All that the Christ self requires of you is that which is the easiest and the most natural for you to give—love. The universal principle active in all of life that may be called karma, the law of mind action, or cause and effect—strong and absolute as it may be—cannot resist love. Love the Lord, Truth, good, and the bonds of past error thought and action begin to fall from your life like paper chains. Misdirected love—love of worry, attachment to the material, self-centeredness—has bound human beings in the cycle of necessary growth experiences. But when love

becomes rightly directed toward the Lord, the wholeness of Spirit that results leaves no room for the past
feelings of weakness or lack. A boy will be content to
play with his toys for a while, but eventually he
begins to miss his mother; when at last he looks up
and sees her, he drops the toys and runs to the
mother's arms. Come to this point in longing, feel
this love as you center your mind on this Father-
Mother, perfect Teacher, Presence indwelling.

Listen, for the Teacher speaks to you in these
moments. The Physician touches you with healing,
the Master touches you with light. Veils fall from
your eyes, sensitivities quicken, as you receive your
own personal spiritual message. If you do not receive
this feeling of communion at first, do not give up.
Try again and again; release yourself completely to
the inner Teacher. Feel that you are truly cleansed,
baptized with light. This experience, you will find, is
not imagination—although imagining the inner
Master and the nature of spiritual communion will
help to prepare your mind and heart for the real experience. The message of Spirit, the realization of the
inner Teacher, will certainly happen to you.

As you contemplate this inner Presence, think of
its radiance flooding your mind and heart. Begin to
see how beautifully and easily the light of spiritual
awareness flows into your consciousness as you
breathe in. Think of the Source of inner light—the
Christ self. Then as you breathe out, think of the
natural outflow, the full expression of Spirit as the
ego-self becomes suffused with the Christ light. The

mind forgets its identification with the space-time, personality self for this eternal moment and identifies with the I AM, the Christ. Hold the idea of this cleansing radiance for a moment, and feel the total healing release of the Christ light shining through your being. Know that this experience is God's love in action in and through you. It is your own Teacher's gift to you.

As you continue to practice this process, ideas of great and special meaning will come to you. Those special, private blessings that you receive from the inner Master shall be your secrets. If words are given to you, they are for you only. If symbols or scenes appear to the inner eye, they are yours alone. They are your treasures.

But the peace you feel, the free, full experience of spiritual joy that comes in this activity is Spirit's gift to all the world through you. Let it flow forth in healing thoughts for all people, in words of praise for the good abundant in people and situations around you. These are the gifts of Spirit outflowing through you; they cleanse and bless you as they flow on to uplift others and this world.

Whenever you undergo times of doubt or dryness in life, turn again to this inner Counselor. Think again of the Master seated in your heart of hearts. Think of the Christ as the very heart of your heart. Contemplate this purity, this peace. Here, there can be no bitterness, no resentment, no remembrance of past wrong. Here is the sacred place of perfect peace, free and unrestrained love, absolute acceptance, ever new beginnings. In these moments of contemplation you shall be comforted and all Truth shall be opened unto you.

Perhaps you will put down these pages after finishing your reading today and still not consciously follow the steps in Self-knowledge that await you in your soul growth. But you cannot pause for long.

You were born for this journey and you never really leave this path. You have given your heart to Truth, you belong to the Christ, your own indwelling Teacher. Be at peace, for the Teacher is with you here, guiding your footsteps, leading you safely and certainly to the spiritual goal of Self-knowledge.

Printed U.S.A.

144-F-3660-15M-10-79